Abraham Coles, Jonathan Ackerman Coles, Ezra Mundy Hunt

Abraham Coles

Biographical Sketch, Memorial Tributes and Selections from his Works

Abraham Coles, Jonathan Ackerman Coles, Ezra Mundy Hunt

Abraham Coles
Biographical Sketch, Memorial Tributes and Selections from his Works

ISBN/EAN: 9783743329133

Manufactured in Europe, USA, Canada, Australia, Japa

Cover: Foto ©ninafisch / pixelio.de

Manufactured and distributed by brebook publishing software (www.brebook.com)

Abraham Coles, Jonathan Ackerman Coles, Ezra Mundy Hunt

Abraham Coles

ABRAHAM COLES:

BIOGRAPHICAL SKETCH,

MEMORIAL TRIBUTES,

SELECTIONS FROM HIS WORKS,

(SOME HITHERTO UNPUBLISHED.)

EDITED BY HIS SON

JONATHAN ACKERMAN COLES, A.M., M.D.

ILLUSTRATED.

NEW YORK:
D. APPLETON & COMPANY.
1892

COPYRIGHT, 1892, BY
JONATHAN ACKERMAN COLES.

NEWARK, N. J.
ADVERTISER PRINTING HOUSE,
1892

DEDICATED

TO

THE EVANGELICAL ALLIANCE,

"AN ASSOCIATION
FOR THE DEFENSE OF RELIGIOUS LIBERTY
AND PROMOTING
THE UNITY OF ALL BELIEVERS
IN THE ESSENTIALS OF CHRISTIANITY
AND THEIR
CO-OPERATION FOR ITS PROGRESS."

"Unum corpus sumus in Christo."

"*Non valet, haec ego dico, haec tu dicis, haec ille dicit— sed haec dicit Dominus.*"—AUGUSTINE.

"Rev. Josiah Strong,
 "General Secretary,
"Rev. Frank Russell,
 "Field Secretary.

"THE EVANGELICAL ALLIANCE,
 "For the United States of America,
  "117 Bible House,

"New York, 30 Dec., 1891.

"Dear ———

"Deerhurst, Scotch Plains, N. J.:

"My esteemed colleague, Dr. Strong, was called to Iowa as your favor of recent date reached the office. He desired me to name its subject matter to some of the members of our Executive Committee, and then to answer you accordingly. I have done so, and only express their pleasure, as well as that of Dr. Strong, when I say that we should all be very glad to have the Alliance honored with the dedication of the book, as it was always honored by the word and deed of your justly eminent father.

"May I add that I have become personally much interested in the book, and shall be glad when the copy reaches the office.

"In behalf of Dr. Strong,

"Most truly yours,

"Frank Russell."

CONTENTS.

DEDICATION, - - - - - - Page iii

LETTER FROM THE EVANGELICAL ALLIANCE, - Page iv

LIST OF ILLUSTRATIONS, - - - - Page xv

SUBJECTS DISCUSSED AT THE GENERAL CHRISTIAN CONFERENCES OF THE WORLD'S ALLIANCE, - - - Pages xix–xlvi

THE SHEPHERD OF THE NATIONS, - - - - Page xxi

THE MESSIAH, - - - - - - Pages xxii–xxiii

"O most illustrious of the days of time!

BREATH OF LIFE, NATURAL AND SPIRITUAL—(From "The Microcosm,") - - - - - - - Page xxiv

"God breathed, O breath with heavenly sweetness rife!
Into man's nostrils first the breath of life."

THEOPNEUSTY—(From "The Microcosm,") - Page xxv

"O via sacra, O thrice blessed door,
Once hallowed with Thy presence, hallow Lord! once more."

GOD IN NATURE—(From "Cosmos,") - - - Page xxvi

MORNING HYMN—(From "Cosmos,") - - Page xxvii

THE UNSEARCHABLE RICHES OF CHRIST, - - Page xxviii

THE BIBLE, - - - - - - - Page xxix

THE FATHERHOOD OF GOD, - - - - - Page xxix

CONTENTS.

REASON AND FAITH, - - - - - Page xxx
CHRIST SUITED TO ALL CHARACTERS, - - - Page xxxi
UNITY OF THE ORIGIN OF MANKIND, - - Page xxxi
THE SOVEREIGNTY OF MAN," - - - - Page xxxiii
CHRISTIAN LEGISLATION, - - - - Page xxxiii
CHRISTIAN EDUCATION, - - - - Page xxxviii
    Columbus.
CHRIST'S LOVE FOR CHILDREN, - - - Page xlii
CHRISTIAN LOVE, - - - - - - Page xliii
    From a letter to George MacDonald.
CHRISTIAN ACTIVITY, - - - - - Page xliv
    From a letter to the Rev. Dr. Cuyler.
CHRISTIAN ASSURANCE, - - - - Page xlvi

BIOGRAPHICAL SKETCH OF ABRAHAM COLES,
  by Ezra M. Hunt, M. D., LL. D., - Pages 1–20

  Birth; parents; the ancestral farm; Dennis Coles; Shepard Kollock; "The Recorder of the Times," - - - Page 2

  School days; teacher of Latin and mathematics; enters as a student the law office of Chief Justice Hornblower, - Page 4

  Studies medicine; attends lectures at the College of Physicians and Surgeons, N. Y., and graduates from the Jefferson Medical College, Philadelphia, 1835; makes a profession of his Christian faith; settles in Newark, N. J., for the practice of medicine and surgery, - - - - - - Page 5

  His fondness for the classics; his marriage; the death of his wife; sails for Europe; the French Revolution of 1848, - - - - - - - - - Page 6

  His literary and professional standing in 1849; again visits Europe, 1854, - - - - - - - Page 7

CONTENTS.

The laying out and beautifying of Deerhurst; the residence, labyrinth and paddock for deer, - - - - Page 8
"The Microcosm," the physiological poem delivered as President of the Medical Society of New Jersey, at its centennial anniversary, - - - - - - Page 10
Honorary degrees received from Rutgers, Lewisburg University and College of New Jersey, Princeton, - Page 12
La Grippe; California; his death, - - Page 13-14
His versions of the "Dies Iræ" and other Latin hymns;
Page 15
"The Evangel," and "The Light of the World;" Page 16
Unpublished manuscripts, - - - - Page 16
"A New Rendering of the Hebrew Psalms into English Verse," - - - - - - - - - Page 17
His respectful bearing toward all; his fondness for little children; his belief in his profession, - - Pages 18-20
His admiration for Abraham Lincoln, - - Page 33

SELECTIONS FROM MEMORIAL TRIBUTES, - Pages 21-78

In Memoriam, Theophilus Bond; "Newark Daily Advertiser;" "Union County Standard;" New York "Tribune;" Essex County Medical Society; Drs. G. R. Kent, Arthur Ward, Joseph D. Osborne, Joseph C. Young, - - Pages 22-27
Funeral services at the Homestead on Market street and at the Church; Rev. Dr. A. H. Burlingham; Rev. Dr. W. W. Boyd; Prof. Edward M. Bowman; New Jersey Historical Society; Rev. Dr. Parks; Rev. Dr. Lowry; Mr. James Sauvage; Rev. Charles F. Deems, D. D.; Rev. George Dana Boardman, D. D.; Rev. Dr. MacArthur; Vice-Chancellor A. V. Van Fleet; Judge David A. Depue; ex-Chancellor Theodore Runyon; the Hon. Amzi Dodd; Hon. Thomas N. McCarter; Hon. Cortlandt Parker; Hon. A. Q. Keasbey; Hon. Frederick W. Ricord, Alexander H.

CONTENTS.

Ritchie, William Rankin, Charles Kyte, Noah Brooks, Edmund C. Stedman, Wilson Schoch, L. Spencer Goble, Dr. S. H. Pennington, Dr. A. W. Rogers, Dr. Ezra M. Hunt, Dr. B. L. Dodd, Dr. J. C. Young, Dr. T. H. Tomlinson, - Pages 28-37

Rev. Robert S. MacArthur, D. D.; Rev. Theodore L. Cuyler, D. D.; Rev. Philip Schaff, D. D.; Rev. Richard S. Storrs, D. D.; James Russell Lowell; Mrs. Mabel Lowell Burnett; William Dean Howells; Justice Bradley, of the United States Supreme Court; Alexander H. Ritchie; Dr. S. H. Pennington; Hon. A. Q. Keasbey; Dr. A. W. Rogers; Noah Brooks; Rt. Rev. Michael A. Corrigan, Roman Catholic Archbishop; J. Marron Dundas, of Philadelphia; Hon. John Wanamaker, Postmaster General; John G. Whittier; Dr. Oliver Wendell Holmes, - - - - Pages 38-46

Mrs. Benjamin Harrison; Mrs. Julia Ward Howe; Mrs. Florence Howe Hall; Mrs. Julia Parmly Billings; Hon. Cortlandt Parker; Rev. Robert Lowry, D. D.; Rev. James McCosh, D. D., of Princeton; Richard W. Gilder; Rev. Wayland Hoyt, D. D.; "The Critic," New York; Frederick W. Ricord; Rev. Wendell Prime, D. D.; Mary J. Porter; Rev. Edward P. Terhune, D. D.; Marion Harland, Pages 47-56

Rev. George M. Van Derlip, Century Association, New York; Rev. Charles S. Robinson, D. D.; Gen. Theodore Runyon; Rev. Henry Clay Trumbull, D. D.; Hiram H. Tichenor, M. D.; the "New York Observer;" Rev. T. E. Vassar, D. D.; Rev. A. H. Lewis, D. D.; Rev. A. H. Burlingham, D. D.; J. K. Hoyt; Rev. J. M. Stevenson, D. D.; Vice-Chancellor A. V. Van Fleet; Rev. Edgar M. Levy, D. D.; Rev. D. J. Yerkes, D. D.; Prof. Robert T. S. Lowell, D. D.; Mary A. Lowell; Hon. Judge David A. Depue; Hon. and Mrs. J. S. T. Stranahan; Grace Aspinwall Bowen; Margaret E. Sangster; Rev. Edwin W. Rice, D. D., - Pages 57-65

Rev. F. M. McAllister; Rev. Alexander McLaren, D. D.; Rev. J. W. Sarles, D. D.; Rev. George E. Horr, D. D.; Rev.

CONTENTS.

Samuel R. House, M. D., D. D.; William Rankin; Rev. Robert P. Kerr, D. D.; Aaron M. Powell, of the Society of Friends; Richard J. Dunglison, M. D.; Rev. John Hall, D. D.; Rev. Abraham Coles Osborn, D. D.,   -   - . Pages 66–70

Bishop John H. Vincent, D. D.; Rev. W. C. Stitt, D. D.; Mrs. Mary Mapes Dodge; Edmund C. Stedman; Prof. William G. Blaikie; Rev. Edward Judson, D. D.; Edward Bierstadt; Rev. Josiah Strong, D. D.; Rev. Henry M. Sanders, D. D.; Rev. D. R. Frazer, D. D.; Rev. H. W. Ballantine, D. D.; E. A. Von Diezelski; Rev. Lyman Abbott, D. D., Pages 70–73

Rt. Rev. John Williams, D. D., Bishop of the Diocese of Connecticut; Rt. Rev. Phillips Brooks, Bishop of the Diocese of Massachusetts; Rev. Benjamin Griffith, D. D.; Nathan Haskell Dole; Elizabeth G. Shepard, "Boston Transcript,"   -   -   -   -   -   -   - Page 74–78

ADDITIONAL SELECTIONS FROM THE WRITINGS OF DR. COLES.

A New Year's Greeting,   -   -   -   -   Page 81

Harmony,   -   -   -   -   -   - Page 83
  "He fails in everything who fails in Love."

The Redeemer,   -   -   -   -   -   - Page 84
  "The Saviour's advent to this far-off earth,
  Who came that He might bring the lost one back."

The Future Life,   -   -   -   -   - Page 88
  "The hour of birth into another life!
  Sooner or later it must come to all."

Hymns for Whitsunday,   -   -   -   -   Page 95

CONTENTS.

VENI CREATOR SPIRITUS—Translation, - - Page 96

VENI SANCTE SPIRITUS—Translation, - Page 97

THE SOWER, - - - - - Page 99

FOREFATHERS' DAY, - - - - - Page 100

    Read before the New England Society of Newark, N. J., on the occasion of the anniversary of the landing of the Pilgrim Fathers on Plymouth Rock, Dec. 10, 1620, O. S.

THE SCOTCH PLAINS, - - - - Page 109

    "From Scotland the first settlers came—"

RETURN AFTER ABSENCE, - - - - Page 115

    "I tread once more my native Plain."

PRAYER IN AFFLICTION, - - - - Page 119

    "Since dust to Deity may speak,
    I come, O God! with bleeding breast."

ON THE DEATH OF PRESIDENT GARFIELD, Page 125

    "The Nation's choice, the Nation's chief,
    Who was so long in dying."

HORACE—GARFIELD, - - - - - Page 128

    NON OMNIS MORIAR! Carmen XXX, Liber III.

    "I've reared a monument alone
    More durable than brass or stone."

TRANSLATIONS OF HORACE, - - - Page 131

    Liber II, Carmen XX.—AD MÆCENATEM.
    Liber I, Carmen XXIV.—AD VIRGILIUM.

CONTENTS.

PARIS IN 1848 AND 1871, - - - - Page 137
    A personal experience.

ROME, ITALY. 1854, - - - - - Page 145
    Mrs. Crawford's agreeable soirees; Hon. and Mrs. Wm. B. Kinney, Florence; Robert and Elizabeth Barrett Browning; Hiram Powers and his busts of "Eve" and "Charity."

WINDERMERE, - - - - - - Page 147

NIAGARA, - - - - - - - Page 149

URBS CŒLESTIS SYON, (Bernard of Cluny), Page 150
    THE BETTER COUNTRY—Translation.

> "The Life here below so brief is brief woe,
>   A brief mortal space for weeping afforded;
> Not briefly to sigh, then lie down and die,
>   Is the life that's to be hereafter awarded."

PROEM, (from "The Evangel,") - - Page 161

> "Spirit Divine, the adding up of gifts,
>   Communicable Godhead, be my guest."

    The Rt. Hon. W. E. Gladstone; Rev. Stephen Gladstone; Science; Evolution.

"IN THE BEGINNING WAS THE WORD (THE LOGOS), AND THE WORD WAS WITH GOD, AND THE WORD WAS GOD," - - - - Pages 167–172
    The first Christians, Platonists, the Ebionites, the Gnostics, Arianism, Ebionism, Marcionism (Docetic Gnosticism), Sabellianism, Apollinarianism, Nestorianism; Eutychianism and Monothe-

litism or Monophysitism, as well as the Lutheran doctrine of the ubiquity of Christ's body; Creeds, Confessions and Christologies; the Trinity.

THE SERVANTS OF THE PEN, - - - Page 172

THE SON OF THE LAW, - - Pages 173-183

    Christ's Infancy and Childhood to the age of twelve, and of the intervening years up to thirty; the Apocryphal and Canonical Gospels; the Apollo Belvedere; Renan, Rousseau; Strauss' boasted "apparatus for causing the miracles of the evangelic history to evaporate into myths."

JOHN THE BAPTIST, - - - - - Page 183

    The Rev. William R. Williams, D. D.

THE BAPTISM, - - - - Pages 185-188

    "God sent thee to baptize, and it is fit
    That I should ratify and thou submit."

"JUDGE NOT," - - - - - Pages 189-190

    The salvation of infants and the heathen.

THAT ALL MEN SHOULD HONOR THE SON, EVEN AS
    THEY HONOR THE FATHER, - - Pages 191-201

    Christ's consciousness of the fact that He was both God and Man.

EPITHALAMIUM, - - - - - - Page 202

THE MARRIAGE IN CANA, - - Pages 204-211

CONTENTS. xiii

WINE AND NEW WINE, - - - Pages 212–219
   Rev. C. H. Spurgeon and unfermented wine.

FAREWELL: LAND OF GENNESARET, - Pages 220–226

PORTAS VESTRAS ÆTERNALES—Translation, Page 227

THE RESURRECTION, - - - - Pages 229–244

REGENERATION, - - - - - Page 245
   "'The lips of Truth to all declare,
    'Ye must be born again.'"

THE MANY MANSIONS, - - - Pages 248–251
   The Lord's Supper.

EUCHARISTIC HYMN, - - - - - Page 252

HARK! CHERUB VOICES SAY, - - - Page 253

DIES IRÆ—17th version, - - - - Page 255

DIES IRÆ—18th version, - - - - Page 259

THE NEW JERUSALEM, - - . - - Page 263

WORKS OF ABRAHAM COLES. - - - Page 269

CRITICS AND CRITICISMS, - - - Page 273
   Richard Grant White; Rev. Samuel Irenæus Prime, D. D.; Wm. Cullen Bryant; James Russell Lowell; "Christian Quarterly Review;" "The Boston Transcript;" Lady Jane Franklin; William C. Prime; Rev. Philip Schaff, D. D.; "The Republican," Springfield; George Ripley, the New York "Tribune;" Rev. James

McCosh, D. D.; Hon. Richard Stockton Field; Newark "Advertiser;" Edmund C. Stedman; Rev. Robert Turnbull, D. D.; John G. Whittier; Rev. S. I. Prime, D. D.; George Ripley, New York "Tribune;" Rev. James McCosh, D. D.

Gov. Daniel Haines; Rev. George Dana Boardman, D. D.; Rev. Charles Hodge, D. D.; Hon. Frederick Theodore Frelinghuysen; Prof. Robert Lowell, D. D.; Prof. Stephen Alexander; Oliver Wendell Holmes; William Cullen Bryant; Chancellor Henry Woodhull Green; Charles H. Spurgeon.

Hon. William Earl Dodge; Thomas Gordon Hake, M. D.; New York "Observer;" the New York "Times;" "The Critic;" John Y. Foster; Hon. Justin McCarthy; the "Examiner and Chronicle;" Hon. Horace N. Congar; Rev. William Hague, D. D.; Newark "Advertiser;" Rev. George Dana Boardman; Rev. A. S. Patton, D. D.; Hon. Joseph P. Bradley; John G. Whittier.

The Rt. Hon. John Bright, M. P.; Rev. H. G. Weston, D. D.; Rev. Horatius Bonar, D. D.; Rev. Alexander McLaren, D. D.; Adele M. Fielde; Elizabeth C. Kinney; "The Book Buyer," Charles Scribner's Sons; Rev. Theodore L. Cuyler, D. D.; the New York "Tribune;" Rev. Frederic W. Farrar, D. D., F. R. S.; Rev. A. H. Tuttle, D. D.; Rev. Charles S. Robinson, D. D.; Hon. George Hay Stuart; Rev. D. R. Frazer, D. D.; Charles M. Davis; Rev. A. H. Lewis, D. D.; S. W. Kershaw, F. S. A.; J. K. Hoyt; Rev. George Dana Boardman, D. D.; Rev. Lewis R. Dunn, D. D.; Rev. Asahel C. Kendrick, D. D.; George MacDonald; Rev. Philip Schaff, D. D.

ILLUSTRATIONS.*

STEEL ENGRAVING OF DR. ABRAHAM COLES,
 by Alexander Hay Ritchie, - - Frontispiece

DEERHURST, - - - - - -

RESIDENCE, viewed from the West, - - Page 1

THE FRONT LAWN, - - - - - Page 7
 Showing the Centennial (1876) marble Italian Vase, the Maidenhair (gingko) and beech-tent trees, etc.

SOME OF THE DEER—THE YOUNG HUNTERS, Page 8

FAC-SIMILE PLAN OF THE HAMPTON COURT LABYRINTH,
 NEAR LONDON, - - - - - - Page 20
 In front of the entrance, Euterpe, an imported copy of the original antique statue in the Berlin Museum.

THE FLOWER GARDEN, - - - - Page 50

THE LIBRARY, - - - - - Page 55

THE DRAWING ROOM, - - - - - Page 77
 Showing portion of the marble copy of the Warwick Vase; bust of Walter Scott; the marble statue of " The Village Blacksmith," by

---

* The illustrations, with the exception of the steel engraving and the view of the deer, were photographed by Mr. Edward Bierstadt himself, he, as a friend, having visited Deerhurst for the purpose. His picture of the flower garden has received particular praise from those acquainted with the Science and Art of Photography.

xvi LIST OF ILLUSTRATIONS.

Shakspere Wood, Rome, 1864; the marble bust of "Charity," by Hiram Powers, and in the centre "Deborah," by Lombardi.

The bust of Scott, of the purest white marble, was purchased of Sypher & Co., New York, and is an exact fac-simile of the one at Abbotsford. John Gibson Lockhart says that " this bust (by Sir Francis Chantrey) alone preserves for posterity the cast of expression most fondly remembered by all who ever mingled in his domestic circle. * * * * Sir Francis Chantrey presented the original bust to Sir Walter himself, by whose remotest descendants it will undoubtedly be held in additional honor on that account. The poet had the further gratification of learning that three copies were executed in marble before the original quitted the studio—one for Windsor Castle, a second for Apsley House, and a third for the friendly sculptor's own private collection."

PORTIONS OF DRAWING ROOM AND MAIN HALL, Page 146

Showing on the left the marble bust of "Charity," by Hiram Powers; and "St. Paul, by Barbee, a bas-relief marble copy of an antique medallion." In the right-hand corner is the life-size bronze bust of Benjamin Franklin, signed "Houdon, 1778." It was purchased of Sypher & Co., New York, whose agent obtained it in Paris. Further to the right are seen the marble bust of "Eve," by Hiram Powers, and the marble copy of the Warwick Vase. In the centre of the room is "Deborah," that "great dame of Lapidoth," as Tennyson calls her, *mulier splendorum, i. e.*, one divinely illuminated. It was executed at Rome in 1875 by the distinguished sculptor, Lombardi,* and constitutes his masterpiece. She is made life-size, of the purest white marble; stands on a storied pedestal with explanatory scenes carved in bas-relief, having the left breast

* In the Sculpture Department of Art, International Exhibition, Philadelphia, Pa., U. S. A., 1876, an object of admiration and interest was Lombardi's beautiful marble group representing a mother-hen with her brood of little chickens, aptly illustrative of Matthew xxiii: 37.

uncovered and right arm uplifted; a beautiful and serious face, expressive of the loftiest enthusiasm and the sacred inspiration of prophetic passion; open lips that need not voice to thrill us with the fiery recital of that grandest of epinician odes, the "Song of Deborah," recorded in the fifth chapter of the Book of Judges, in which is commemorated the wonderful victory of a small portion of her people over Sisera, the Captain of the Canaanitish host, and the deliverance of all Israel from twenty years' servitude—the whole achieved mainly by the high courage and heroic instigation of this noble woman, who was essentially a *vates*, combining the functions of poetry and prophecy. On this glorious triumphal ode much has been written, and there are separate treatises about it. All agree in regarding it as a magnificent specimen of primitive Hebrew poetry. The artist was fortunate in his subject. But to justify his choice he would need to have the consciousness of powers equal to it. No doubt it was a bold attempt to carve breath, to make marble alive and splendidly lyrical, to perpetuate a speaking rapture—in other words, to produce a "Deborah" in stone, which should not be unworthy of the historic reality. This, judges and critics think he has done.

The Last Hours of Mozart - - Page 258
From a photograph of the original painting by Kaulbach.

Amelia Gere Mason, in "The Century Magazine," (Dec., 1891), says: "Mozart, in his last letter to a friend, wrote, 'I regard the future without fear or terror. I feel that my hour is about to strike. I touch the limits of my life. I am going to die before having enjoyed the fruits of my talent. * * * It will be as it pleases God; as for myself, I must finish my funeral hymn. * * * 'Ah! Sophie,' he said to his sister-in-law, whom he had thoughtfully asked to stay with Constance (his wife) the last night of his life, 'did I not tell you that I was writing the Requiem for my own funeral?' A few hours before the end he joined the friends in singing the parts already finished, and died with the score beside him.' 'As death, taken all in all, is the true end of life,' he said in his last letter to his father four years before, 'I have grown so familiar for a couple of years with this real and devoted friend, that its aspect, far from inspiring me with terror and fear, offers me only consoling thoughts and sweet hopes. I thank God for having accorded to me the favor of looking upon it as the key to our veritable beatitude.' * * *

"In one corner of the cemetery of St. Marx (Vienna) stands today a solitary monument. A pedestal of gray granite is surmounted by the bronze figure of a Muse sitting upon a pile of books bearing the names of Mozart's principal works. In her left hand she holds a harp, which rests upon a wreath of laurel hung carelessly over the books, while the right hand grasps the score of 'Dies Iræ.' The head droops in pity, and the face is unutterably sad. The four corners of the base bear each a candelabrum twined with laurel. The front of the pedestal has a bronze relief of the composer, and the rear a wreathed harp. On one side is written 'Wolfgang Amadeus Mozart, born January 27, 1756; died, December 5, 1791.' Nearly seventy years after his death this tardy tribute was erected over his supposed burial-place."

SUBJECTS DISCUSSED AT THE GENERAL

CHRISTIAN CONFERENCES OF THE

WORLD'S ALLIANCE.

The Lord taketh pleasure in his people, he will beautify the meek with salvation.—*Psalms cxlix: 4.*

Blessed are the meek, for they shall inherit the earth.—*Matthew v: 5.*

THE meek of every name may boast
    The adoption of the Holy Ghost;
And lift an unpresuming eye
To God, and Abba, Father, cry.
Therefore by Church be understood
A high and holy brotherhood.

In faithful league let all unite,
And serve the Lord with all their might!
Compared with love count names but dross!
Drawn by th' attraction of the Cross,
In peaceful circles round it run
Like planets moving round the sun!

THE SHEPHERD OF THE NATIONS.

I SING the Shepherd of the sheep,
   Who saw, in times of old,
Of all the worlds that roam the deep,
   One wanderer from the fold.

I sing the love, so strange, so sweet,
   That sought until it found;
With aching heart and bleeding feet
   And tears that wet the ground.

I sing the goodness of our God;
   The patience and the grace;
That left no dreadful path untrod
   To save the human race.

The Shepherd of the nations, He
   His gathered flock shall guide—
The travail of His soul shall see
   And shall be satisfied.

THE MESSIAH.

"Unto us a child is born, unto us a son is given: and the government shall be upon his shoulder; and his name shall be called Wonderful, Counsellor, The Mighty God, The Everlasting Father, The Prince of Peace."—ISAIAH IX: 6.

O MOST illustrious of the days of time!
  Day full of joy and benison to earth,
When Thou wast born, sweet babe of Bethlehem!
With dazzling pomp descending, angels sung
Good will and peace to men, to God due praise,
Who on the errand of salvation sent
Thee, Son Beloved! of plural Unity
Essential part, made flesh that mad'st all worlds.
  Ay, well and gloriously didst Thou achieve
Thy god-like mission, both by life and death.
Light broke upon the nations; at Thy word
Roused from the sleep of ages. Truths long lost,
Man's immortality and higher life,
The unity and fatherhood of God,
The splendid verities of Christian Faith,
Ran swiftly and were glorified in every land.

Thy Universal Empire, whose sole law
Is Love, rose silently, and without violence
Freeing from old oppression. Ne'er till them
Did man know aught of Freedom, or could know.
The sensual and depraved are slaves perforce.
The free of soul, the pure, the sanctified,
Alone are free, the Freemen of the Lord,—
True King of Christendom, whose gracious sway,
None shares.
   * * * * * *

"One is your Master," saith our Head, "even Christ,
And there results to you equality
Of brotherhood. Humility is rank;
The least is greatest and the greatest least."

BREATH OF LIFE, NATURAL AND SPIRITUAL.

[FROM "THE MICROCOSM."]

GOD breathed, O breath with heavenly sweetness rife!
    Into man's nostrils first the breath of life.
The blissful aura vivified the whole,
And straightway man became a living soul.
Then odorous Eden yet more odorous grew,
As o'er its bowers, th' informing spirit blew
Another inner and diviner air,
Moving within the proper atmosphere,
That shook the leaves and made the tree-tops nod,
A mystic wind immediately from God,—
Rushing and mighty like the Holy Ghost
Poured out upon the day of Pentecost.
Still the same Spirit where it lists it blows,
We know not whence it comes nor where it goes,
But souls it quickened on Creation's morn,
Now dead in sin to a new life are born:
One inspiration of immortal breath
Creates a life beneath the ribs of death.

THEOPNEUSTY.

[FROM "THE MICROCOSM."]

O VIA SACRA, O thrice blessed door,
   Once hallowed with Thy presence, hallow, Lord!
      once more.
Imbreathe Thyself, my Maker! fill each cell
Of my deep breast, and deign with me to dwell.
Come, my Desire! Thou theme of heavenly tongues,
Fulfill the want and hunger of the lungs.
Be Thou my breath, my laughter, my delight,
My song by day, my murmured dream by night.
When hope dilates, and love my bosom warms,
Be these the product of Thy powerful charms.
If grief convulses, be it grief for sin,
Prompt every sigh and make me pure within;
Perfumed by Thee "make every breath a spice
And each religious act a sacrifice."

GOD IN NATURE.

[FROM "COSMOS."]

To see with eyes of wonder, and with heart
    Of worship, God, in all—the Mystery,
That renders sacred most familiar things—
With priestly ministrations here to stand
In the grand Temple of the Universe,
Voicing the praises of all creatures mute,
This is Religion, and for this alone
Was man created sovereign of the world.

    Yea! all things are of God. This infinite
And unimaginable Universe,
Built up of atoms, hath no other Cause,
No other Father. His utterable Will
Is the foundation on which Nature rests.
God underlieth every meanest grain;
There, even there, is His omnipotence
And love and wisdom, else it could not be.

MORNING HYMN.

STANZAS 2, 8 AND 9.

[FROM "COSMOS."]

L OWLY in attitude,
  Musical gratitude
Fain would I pour to Thee fervent and sweet—
  Thank Thee in verity,
  Bless in sincerity,
Wonder, and worship, and wait at Thy feet.

  Type of Divinity!
  Over infinity
Throwing a mantle of beauty and light;
  Life of the perishing,
  Cheering and cherishing,
Blazon His goodness and wisdom and might!

  Earth! in simplicity,
  Sing thy felicity,
Bosomed in azure, and bride of the sky;
  Favored and beautiful,
  No more undutiful,
Low at His footstool contentedly lie!

THE UNSEARCHABLE RICHES OF CHRIST.

Ephesians III : 8.

O THE unsearchable riches of Christ!
    Wondrous, mysterious treasure,
Riches of wisdom past finding out,
    Riches of grace without measure.

O the unsearchable riches of Christ!
    Riches of love and salvation,
Riches of glory unspeakably bright,
    Shaming the starry creation.

O the unsearchable riches of Christ!
    Price of an infinite pardon,
Payment in full of the debt of the race,
    Forfeit incurred in the garden.

O the unsearchable riches of Christ!
    Title to all things possessing,
Worthy the Lamb, let us sing, to receive,
    Riches and honor and blessing.

—*From "The Microcosm and Other Poems."*

THE BIBLE.

The Bible is a venerable book. Most venerable. For four thousand years as a part or a whole it has been "a road through the abyss of time," upon which men have walked as if it were solid pavement. It is the only bridge spanning the gulf, buttressed, and upheld by divine veracity. Beneath it hell yawns. Faith goes up upon it, singing. Rainbows of Hope and Promise hover over it. Everlasting Joy and Blessedness beckon at the end. There always is light when everywhere else is darkness; ever and anon God's smile breaking through; death itself no longer dreadful—

"Only a gray eve 'tween two shining days;"

a comma betwixt this and that, betwixt two existences, yet one, betwixt time and eternity, betwixt earth and heaven. Receiving it as God's Gift-Book, Keepsake, Souvenir; how delightful to turn its pages, filled with testimonies of His love, odorous with His breath, musical with His voice! * * * *

THE FATHERHOOD OF GOD.

I am affected by the spirit of the time. But I am faithful to my allegiance to the Bible. It is that or nothing. Nothing but that speaks with authority, or throws any light upon man's destiny. Science is a fool when it discusses origins, or treats of the mysteries of the beyond. My creed is born, as I suppose most others to be, of a felt need. An atoning Saviour meets that need as nothing else does. I feel myself guilty, and that provides pardon. God is love. The highest proof of it is He gives His Son, and He gives us the spirit of adoption whereby, with yearning affection, we cry, Abba Father. Agnosticism gives us assurance of nothing. It makes the dark darker. Better not to live at all than to live in doubt and ignorance. Existence in that case would be insupportable. An eternity of existence would be an eternity of misery, realizing Buddhist hells innumerable, from which there is no escape save in annihilation. The Lord's Prayer alone is worth a thousand times all the literatures of the world. It is suited to all extremities and all needs. The first word is a sunburst fraught with all comfort—"Our Father." We who are fathers know somewhat what the name of Father implies. If it expresses in us an unutterable tenderness, how much more in the God and Father of our Lord Jesus Christ. * * *

REASON AND FAITH.

The claims of Faith divorced from Reason and pushed too far naturally give rise to rationalistic reactions of an infidel character. An attempt to separate the two, to set one over against the other, as if they were antagonistic, cannot be otherwise than injurious to the cause of true religion and favorable to scepticism. * * * Let us be willing to accept the Bible as it is, believing that all Scripture is given by inspiration of God, and is profitable for doctrine, for reproof, for instruction in righteousness; that holy men spake as they were moved by the Holy Ghost; that apostles were ordained and set apart by a special consecration to make known the way of life and salvation to men. * * * * The declaration that "God so loved the world that He gave His only begotten Son that whosoever believeth on Him should not perish but have everlasting life," is worth more to us than all other knowledge. Let us cling to that! * * * *

CHRIST SUITED TO ALL CHARACTERS.

I think as we grow older our love of speculation diminishes, and we are more inclined to return to the childlike and simple, and make our Christology more trustful than curious. The titular and personal Christ is many-sided, and suited to all characters. The question, What think ye of Christ? whose Son is He? is addressed less to the speculative intellect, than to the inquiring heart amid its tossing disquietudes, seeking rest and finding none. My needs I feel to be manifold and unutterable, and when I pray acocrding to the divine formula, "Give us this day our daily bread," I intend an appeal to the Infinite Helper for infinite help such as my case requires; and I give reverent welcome and entertainment to the gracious invitation, "Come unto Me all ye that labor and are heavy laden and I will give you rest," as divinely authoritative—a veritable "voice from heaven" (bath-kol), with a power and a mission to comfort and save to the uttermost.   *   *   *   *

THE UNITY OF THE ORIGIN OF MANKIND.

To pretend that the Bible is silent, and bears no testimony on the subject of man's origin, is absurd; nay more, it is dishonest. Everybody knows or ought to know better. Or to say, as some are fond of doing, that being an affair of science, its testimony thereon is of no value, is manifestly both foolish and impious. What Revelation formally and expressly teaches must be true, no matter what the subject. It does not teach astronomy, because this does not properly fall within its purview or purpose. But it does teach the creation of man, because it has to do with man; is anthropological in its whole scope and design. It begins at the beginning; shows the tree of human existence at its first planting; shows it to have been one, and that all its boughs and branches, stretching through all lands and all times, proceeded from a single trunk. This common origin of mankind is not doubtfully set forth in a few isolated texts. It is declared or implied in every sentence, in every word of the sacred record. It underlies the whole superstructure. Take it away, and it disjoints and dislocates everything. It is "chaos come again." For human unity is something more than a dead fact; it is a vital truth, out of which grow fundamental doctrines. Therefore we say if the Bible be true, the question is settled; and to the guesses of science there comes this crowning and conclusive certainty. * * * * We are unable to conceive of the Creator as sitting behind His works as a passive spectator—having, a long time ago, as some one remarks, wound up the great machine of the universe, and left Himself nothing further to do but to find amusement in seeing it go. If a sparrow falls not to the ground without His notice, and the hairs of our head are all numbered, why is it absurd to suppose that at the time of the dispersion at Babel, following the confusion of tongues, when under an irresistible impulse towards emigration, the people were scattered abroad over the whole earth, the Hand of God went with them, and impressed upon the plastic nature of man, then in the infancy of his being, such changes as were fitted to accommodate him more speedily and kindly to his new position, mediately or immediately, as you please, either supposition being warrantable? * * * *

THE SOVEREIGNTY OF MAN.

It was intended that the relations between man and nature should be those of sovereign and subject. It was by express appointment that all things were put under him. That the supremacy has not been fully asserted is no fault of Nature. She is not unwilling. She is loyal to her very core. She delights in obedience. We are only beginning to learn the rich possibilities of her service. For the past fifty years we have been going on from wonder to wonder. It is becoming increasingly difficult to say where the natural ends and the supernatural begins. The *modus operandi* of a miracle is unknown to us. How did Christ work miracles? Was it by virtue of a divine power inherent in Him and peculiar to Him? Possibly. But is it not conceivable that, knowing Nature and believing in her, He had command of her infinite resources? All knowledge is free—divine and human. Nature says, Come! Christ says, Come! What future miracles will be wrought as the result of the twofold welcome remains to be seen. We come up close to the borders of the Spirit land. * * * *

CHRISTIAN LEGISLATION.

From a letter to the late Hon. Joseph P. Bradley, LL. D., one of the Justices of the Supreme Court of the United States of America.

Permit me to thank you for sending me your admirable brochure on "Law: Its Nature and Effects as the Bond and Basis of Society." It seems to me to be a very luminous and instructive survey, freeing the subject of much confusion and ambiguity. You may remember that I studied law six months under your honored father-in-law, Judge Hornblower, deceased, during which time I read with considerable attention Blackstone, and Kent's Commentaries. That was more than half a century ago, and while it did not make me a lawyer, it gave me some taste for legal studies. I have never regretted the time thus spent. In reading your pamphlet, I feel more than ever, how much I owe to the laws established, and how thankful I ought to be that I live under their protection. How safe it makes me! far more than an armed guard at my door!

To the loyal and obedient, Law is paternal and benign. It is a shield and a high tower. But not so to its violators. To them it wears a changed aspect, full of dreadful menace. To the end that it may appear to all that it bears not the sword in vain, it is not slow nor slack to punish. It arrests, and brooks no resistance. It consigns to dungeons. It hangs upon the gallows. Can it be that this is the selfsame power that one moment before the crime was committed, was firmly and solemnly pledged for the felon's safe-keeping, protesting that not a hair of his head should be injured? Even so. The Law stands upright, but the transgressor holds towards it an inverted position, and, by virtue of this invertion, he is emptied of all his rights under the law.

You make it very plain that the Law is not simply preceptive; that Law, to be Law, pre-supposes a power and an authority behind it, pledged inevitably, if need be, to a physical enforcement; in other words, it is a command backed by penalty constituting its sanction. You are clearly right, therefore, in saying that Blackstone's definition, *quod hoc*, is defective. Whether, moreover, in seeking to find an analogy between the laws of nature, and municipal laws, he does not paralogize, may perhaps be questioned. Is the law of gravity a command? and do I incur the guilt of disobedience if I make a leap in the air? Metaphorically, it may be true that I am commanded not to leap down a precipice, and not to drink poison. But still, it would seem that there is a difference. May it not have happened that on a fanciful and fallacious analogy of this kind was based the old English law of inheritance, whereby an estate belonging to a deceased intestate was made to descend, gravitation wise, to his uncle or aunt, to the exclusion of his father or other lineal ancestor: "*Descendit itaque jus quasi ponderosum quid cadens deorsum recta linea vil transversati et nunquam reascendit ea via qua descendit.*"

The word *jus* labors under the disadvantage of being equivocal, bifurcating into two senses, meaning sometimes *right* and sometimes *law*, which are not, we are accustomed to think, always the same thing. But if Law be, as you nobly conceive it, a synonym of Justice, then indeed *jus* may be allowed to stand as a pregnant and true representative at once of the ideal and the actual, the abstract and the concrete. In that case, it would follow that a *bad* law is no law. It is like a *bad* Christian, a solecism and a contradiction in terms—a temporary excrescence on the body politic, and no true part of it—to be borne with, it may be, but only until it can be formally rescinded; or, if its unjust character be flagrant and subversive of fundamental law, set aside as of no authority. Thus viewed, no doubt, Law is a majestic thing, whose seat is, as Hooker puts it, "the bosom of God, her voice the harmony of the world," etc.

Just laws have an intrinsic authority, and so have a moral and spiritual enforcement, independent of that which the State supplies. But the civil law, as it has only lately come to be understood, is legitimately confined to the outward and the visible. It lies, to be sure, within the domain of conscience, but does not circumscribe it. It is an *imperium in imperio*. It has been wisely said that "where the Law ends, *Tyranny* begins," but it may be said with equal truth that there *Liberty* begins. Having rendered unto Cæsar the things that are Cæsar's, Conscience is free. There is no form of despotism so detestable as Spiritual Despotism. * * * *

Nevertheless, the State cannot afford to do without the supports of religion. Reverence for law is indissolubly interwoven with reverence for God. Law divorced from the sanctities of religious belief is little better than a horse-whip. It may excite terror, and so far as that restrains, it may restrain, but that is about all. How is it with us? Am I not right in affirming that the State, although it does not formulate its faith, is distinctively Christian, not Pagan, not Mohammetan, not atheistic, not agnostic—however it may tolerate Pagans, Mohammetans, Atheists and Agnostics—all alike being admitted to the immunities of citizenship, and subjected to no disabilities on account of their peculiar religious belief. This is as it should be.

But I believe, with Daniel Webster, that Christianity, general, tolerant Christianity, is a part of the law of the land. The State accepts the Decalogue and builds upon it. As Right presupposes a standard, it assumes that this is such a standard, divinely given, and accepted by all Christendom; that it underlies all civil society, is the foundation of the foundation, is lower than all and higher than all; commends itself to reason; speaks with authority to the Conscience, vindicates itself in all government, giving it stability and exalting it in righteousness; guarantees equities; and proclaimed liberty, equality and fraternity ages before socialism dreamed it, and knew of no other way of effecting it but by pulling down with bloody hands, without any power to build up. While the State is theoretically, at least, "Broad based upon the people's will," God forbid that it should therefore follow that our whole system of laws is at the mercy or whim of a rowdy majority. Suppose it were given out that there would be on a particular day a grand game of tenpins, the pins being the Ten Commandments. All the b'hoys would be sure to be on hand. Bowling Tom hits it at the first throw, and bowling Dick the same, and bowling Harry the same. Give these fellows any sort of a chance, and they will topple over the whole Decalogue for you in no time. * * *

Do you not think there is danger that men's respect for Law will be impaired by the practice of measuring the infinities of justice and right with the uncertain yardstick of an accidental majority? Who are our legislators? Laws passed by a large assembly, are, at best, apt to bear the marks of a hasty and tumultuary origin—incondite and imperfect in form, drawn up by incompetent, it may be, corrupt hands. It is fortunate that all our laws do not emanate from our legislatures. Case-law, proceeding from a wise and learned judiciary, is worthy of all respect—far more so, I should think, than statute law. And yet I should not wonder if some of our judges gave undue weight sometimes to the authority of precedent, out of a superstitious reverence for the old and patristic, like that paid by some churchmen to the Christian fathers. Your foot, I dare say, is as good a standard of measurement as the foot of any Lord Chancellor that ever wore ermine. Why not? Common sense is a thing of the present as well as of the past. It is a pity that all do not estimate law as you do, as a sacred thing, a kind of religion. Law so regarded is a spiritual force, related to celestial dynamics.

I remember when Lincoln's Emancipation Proclamation was first proposed, some said that it would be a *brutum fulmen*. I did not think so. I believed it would be a live thunderbolt, heaven-forged, swift, subtle, far-flaming, far-reaching, irresistible, striking to the centre; and so it proved—"Where the word of a king is, there is power."

You knew, I dare say, the late Judge Joel Jones, of Pennsylvania. He was a firm believer in the Millennium and the personal reign of Christ upon the earth. I am not sure that I am. But, whereas the Atlantic ocean has become, as you say, a ferry, and all walls of partition between the nations are being broken down, and the whole world has become a sort of whispering gallery, there would seem to be no good reason why there should not be, if not now, eventually in the time coming, one system of laws for all peoples, and a fraternal recognition of the solidarity of the race. * * *

CHRISTIAN EDUCATION.

From an address on Religious Education in its Relation to Public Schools and Sunday-schools:

* * * * The Church is Christ's school. Christ is the Master. We who claim to be His disciples, are we His disciples indeed? eager to listen? diligent to learn? never so happy as when sitting at His feet? Are our mounting feet on the rounds of the ladder of a heavenly graduation? * * * Docility becomes teachers no less than scholars. It is their duty to learn in order to teach; and by diligent study of God's Word continue learning until they become workmen that need not to be ashamed. * * * When it pleased God to reveal His Son in us, He did it that we might manifest Him to others who know Him not, by all methods of teaching and holy living. What a privilege! It is as though it were given to human hands to unbar the gates of the morning, and let in the day. And truly, he does more than this, who reveals to the closed eyes of the ignorant the risen orb of the Sun of Righteousness with healing in his wings, irradiating spiritual firmaments and the immensity of heavenly horizons. * * *

"Whatsoever thy hand findeth to do, do it with thy might!" Whatever our hand finds—things that meet us at home, in the family, in our every-day intercourse with our fellow-men, in the Church or in the Sunday-school—let us do these, not pushing aside and repelling these smaller duties, that crowd around us like little children—things that are already found and present—that we may go the world over, hunting for some great thing to do, something which the hand has not found, remote and foreign to us. It is wonderful how much can be accomplished by one who considers the kind of talent he has, the sphere he moves in, and aims to fill it. There is a contagion of goodness. A fire kindled spreads. A handful of corn multiplies into waving harvests. Let us aim at perfection; seek to be best in everything; the best fathers, the best mothers, the best sons, the best daughters, the best scholars, the best teachers, the best in our several callings, and finally, in short, the best Christians and at the same time, the humblest. Let none of us imagine we have a right to be idle in a world where everything is moving. "My Father worketh hitherto and I work," saith our great Exemplar. He was liable to weariness as well as we; but He was always going about doing good. It is a significant and solemn fact that the tree against which Christ sent forth the sentence was not a poisonous tree, not an Upas, but a tree that did nothing. * *

No doubt, the grand secret of efficiency and success is Love! Loving the Word, we will love to teach it. Love will make us eloquent. It will make our looks sweet, our tones musical, our words persuasive. This is what we want. We want, to be sure, faith, but that is pre-supposed. Certainly there should be more than half belief. Our aims should be definite. What is the object we have in view? Have we any object? If not, then most likely will all our labor be thrown away. It will be but a repetition of the feat of shooting at Nothing and hitting it; or the preposterous venture of that eccentric seaman, not since heard from, who, leaving chart and compass behind, set sail long ago for the port of Nowhere. Let us have at least the faith of a Columbus. He believed, and his belief discovered America. He, with his compass and his eye fixed on the pole-star, steered due West, sailing through many weary days and nights, onward, onward, over dark and tempestuous seas unvisited before by any ship's keel; not doubting that the world he sought was there somewhere behind the distant horizon, although he could not see it. * * * *

Religion is a vast social matter. Even in its earthly relations, it is the chief thing. Nothing is so vital as it. It is at once the highest and the lowest. Like the granite which is found, now deep down below the many strata of the overlying rocks, supporting all above it, and then is seen cropping out and towering in the highest mountains. The State cannot afford to be indifferent to that which is the most essential thing of all. If it provides the means of knowledge, it is in an important sense in order to this. For the grand object of knowledge is to make men better. To make men better is to make better citizens. This is what the State aims at. If this be not gained nothing is gained, and the State is without pay or reward for all its labor and loss. Its vast expenditure is mere waste, if not something worse than waste. * * * *

Knowledge is power. But dissociated from virtue, it is power for evil rather than good. It is a curse rather than a blessing. Those who affirm that religious culture is out of place and not permissible in our Public Schools, entirely misconceive the purpose for which these schools were instituted. Undoubtedly, that purpose is mainly and ultimately moral. It is to form the character. To educate the conscience as well as to expand the intellect. To qualify for the business, but still more for the duties of life. It therefore necessarily includes Religion. Duty is nothing without the compelling must of a divine obligation. A morality that has not religion for its root is a pole stuck in the ground, not a tree bearing fruit. The moral side of man is, we know, the divine side. It fronts the infinite. Thereby he is put into indissoluble relation with laws other than physical, and his well-being in time and throughout eternity, made dependent upon their faithful observance. * * * *

In assuming the truth of Christianity, we only follow the State. We assume no more than she assumes. If we are partial in assigning to the Bible a place in our Public Schools, which we refuse to the Koran, the State is partial likewise. In her Halls of Legislation and in her Courts of Justice she recognizes one Divine Book, and appoints that to be used perpetually, as a means of giving validity and solemnity to her acts. It appoints the formality of an oath to be taken on the Bible for the swearing of witnesses; and this is the most usual form; and this thing has a further significance. For not only does the State in this appointment recognize the authority of the Bible, but she virtually obligates herself to provide the means of making those whom she undertakes to educate acquainted with its contents. For, undeniably, the form employed is no better than a solemn mockery, unless the party upon whom it is imposed, knows something of the Book, and accepts it as divine. Consistency therefore requires that the reading, if not the study of the Bible, form a part of the educational course in our schools. At the same time it is not pretended that we can enforce belief. A regulation that makes the Bible a text-book, and the reverent reading of it a daily duty, does not compel any one to believe it. The mind is necessarily free; is not subject to outward constraint; is compelled only by forces which are within itself. We are far from entertaining that grand and fatal fallacy that the cause of religion can be served by outward compulsion; by legal pains and penalties. * * *

Against the inflowings of all error and unbelief, from whatever quarter, the Bible is our only safeguard. Its invincibility has been tried on many a field, and always made good the promise that, *When the enemy shall come in like a flood, the Spirit of the Lord shall lift up a standard against him.* For God is in His Word; and His pervasive presence is the vital secret of its perpetual power and continual triumphs. * * *

Coeval with the dawn of consciousness is the sentiment of duty, and the feeling of accountability. The teaching therefore cannot begin too early. It may properly precede the alphabet. It is as cruel and as criminal to withhold necessary knowledge as to withhold necessary food. Childhood, we know, is singularly receptive— has swift, sure instincts and intuitions outrunning sometimes experience and logic; and ought not therefore to be unduly distrusted. We see the new-born babe perfect from the first in an unlearned art. So likewise in spiritual matters—what is hard for the man is easy for the child. No films of prejudice or doubt cloud the vision. Duty is plain. *I ought* stands clear in the sunlight. * * * *

CHRIST'S LOVE FOR CHILDREN.

From a letter to a little girl, a daughter of the late Judge James Hervey Ackerman.

I thank you very much for the beautiful book-mark you sent me. I confess I don't know a nicer little girl than you are. This is my candid opinion, and I am willing everybody should know it.

CHRISTIAN LOVE.

Tell your dear mother to kiss you on both cheeks for me. Continue to be good. Love the Saviour. When He was on the earth a great while ago, He took little children in His arms and blessed them. I think some of them must have been about your age, and I am quite sure not one of them ever forgot it. Jesus is now in heaven, but He sees and knows all that you say and do. If you ask Him He will bless you too, for nobody loves you so much as He does. When you do wrong you must ask His forgiveness and try not to do so again. Be happy yourself and do all you can (and that is a great deal) to make others happy. Give my love to your mother and your brothers and sister.

CHRISTIAN LOVE.

From a letter to George MacDonald:

Your Christmas remembrances, Novalis and all, mailed on my birthday (please excuse the noticing of the coincidence) came duly to hand, thanks to the postal zeal of two great nations, who, knowing how important is the commerce of fraternity and good will, lend themselves to be our winged Mercuries and servitors to fetch or carry our messages of business or love. I ought, I suppose, to feel like an old man, but I do not. "The trees of the Lord are full of sap," even in winter. I, also, vegetating in the tropics of God's favor, renew my leaf. My heart still burgeons and blooms. I am not sensible of any failure in the power and blessedness of loving. I am as capable of warm friendship as ever. Common friendship is much, but Christian fellowship is more. If I love you for your own sake, I ought to love you with a higher love for Christ's sake. The *homo sum* of Terence is generous, but human; it does not mount to the divine elevation of Christ's "Love one another, as I have loved you." What an infinite dearness is a love which stopped at nothing to save mankind. By feeding on Christ we are converted to a divine sameness and oneness in Him. We eat the same spiritual meat and drink the same spiritual drink, but contrary to what takes place in ordinary alimentation, we do not transubstantiate the food, but the food transubstantiates us. Instead of assimilating, we are assimilated. From this Eucharist of love there results an immense augmentation of the power of loving. Then only can we be said to be perfect in love when we can love all whom Christ loves with an equal love.

I am glad and grateful for your translations. They are marvelously faithful. * * * * What a joy it would be to see you once more. Our hands beckon you. Come. In the meantime, let us live in your remembrance.

CHRISTIAN ACTIVITY.

From a letter to the Rev. Theodore L. Cuyler, D. D.:

One of the most striking of our Lord's Similitudes is that of the Sower: "Behold, a sower went forth to sow." It forms the subject of a picture which has always deeply interested me. Everything is true to life. We admire the cheerful energy of his measured step and the confident swing of his vigorous arm as he sows the seed. I know of no finer exhibition of Trust. At first sight it might seem like thriftless waste, a reckless throwing away of the precious grain, but we know it is not. On the contrary, there is in it shrewd calculation and wise husbandry. * * * * The earth only receives to give back again, multiplied thirty, sixty and a hundredfold. To estimate the greatness of the Divine liberality in this respect, let us take the minimum, calling the rates of increase thirtyfold per annum, and let the multiplication go on for thirty years. Suppose we sow one bushel to the acre—it would form a nice sum in Geometrical Progression to cipher out and tell the number of acres that would be sown, and the number of bushels produced during that period. It is easy to see that the mighty harvest would fill the universe. The Commutation would proceed in this wise:

Time.	Acres sown.	Yield in bushels.
1st year,	1	30
2d year,	30	900
3d year,	900	27,000
4th year,	27,000	810,000
5th year,	810,000	24,300,000
6th year,	24,300,000	729,000,000

It is useless to pursue it further. Now for bushels substitute souls. Suppose you are the means of converting thirty souls a year, and each of these thirty should be the means of converting thirty more, and each of these 900, thirty more, making 27,000 souls, and so on, it would not take long to convert the whole world. Unfortunately, every convert is not a Cuyler, and the work, therefore, goes on slowly.

While sowing the divine seed of the Kingdom has been the main business of your life, and while God has pre-eminently blessed your labors, you have employed, as it were, your moments of rest and recreation in "scattering seeds of kindness" all your life long with an unsparing hand, and I do not believe the harvest has been less abundant because the growing grain has been bordered with flowers, sweet pansies and forget-me-nots. I am not sure that the distinction I make between the seeds of kindness and the seeds of the Kingdom is a just one, for are we not told that the giving of a cup of cold water is a Christian service? I am convinced your kind and loving nature has largely contributed to your success.

* * * * *

CHRISTIAN ASSURANCE.

The night is far spent, the day is at hand. Let us quicken our footsteps. The Lord cometh, and we go forth to meet Him. Let us not doubt but that everything we have committed to Him we shall find safe in His keeping.

Death is a door opening heavenward.

Were it not for death one might be tempted to doubt whether it is really so that God is love.

Death does not terminate friendship, but only seals it and makes it more sacred. It follows our friends into the other world, and has the stamp of immortality fixed upon it. The gate through which they passed stands open. Our tears as they fall are suffused and made iridescent with a heavenly light like rainbows in a shower, for they are tears of joy as well as grief.

Let us not doubt that God has a father's pity towards us, and that in the removal of that which is dearest to us He is still loving and kind. Death separates but it also unites. It reunites whom it separates.

BIOGRAPHICAL SKETCH

OF

ABRAHAM COLES, M. D., Ph. D., LL. D.,

BY

EZRA M. HUNT, M. D., LL. D.

This life, let it be long or short, is but the prefatory chapter of a Life which is yet to be lived, and which is never to end—the initial foreword of an eternal biography.

BIOGRAPHICAL SKETCH.

ABRAHAM COLES, M. D., Ph. D., LL. D., son of Dennis and Catherine (Van Deursen) Coles, was born December 26, 1813, at Scotch Plains, New Jersey. His father was then living on the ancestral farm, which he had inherited, its title-deed antedating the Revolution. He was a man of sterling integrity, sound judgment, and rare literary taste. He had been for a number of years, (after an apprenticeship with Shepard Kollock of Revolutionary fame), a printer and editor in Newburg, N. Y., of a newspaper—"The Recorder of the Times." Bound volumes of this paper were preserved and treasured by his son Abraham, in whom he early cultivated his fondness for study and for literature.

As a youth, Dr. Coles manifested a diligent interest in the acquisition of knowledge. Dr. J. W. Craig, of

Plainfield, once told me that he well remembered his assiduity as a boy, as, from day to day, he saw him coming all the way from Scotch Plains to Plainfield in order to have the advantage of a better school than he could attend at home. Yet his parents do not seem to have looked forward to his special preparation for a professional life, as we find him for two years in a dry-goods store, and as he never entered any college for academic studies. All this time, his love of learning must have led him to private study, for, at the age of seventeen, he assisted Rev. Mr. Bond, pastor of the First Presbyterian Church of Plainfield, in his school, as teacher of Latin and mathematics.

At eighteen years of age, he had resolved to study law, and entered the office of Chief Justice Joseph C. Hornblower, at Newark. He seems soon to have discovered that he could find a wider field for usefulness in the practice of medicine than of law, for, in less than a year, he left the office to study for the medical profession. His resolution to make himself acquainted with law was, however, never shaken. Throughout his long life, his fondness for the law and his knowledge thereof were manifested on many occasions.

Having attended lectures at the College of Physicians and Surgeons, New York, and at Jefferson College, Philadelphia, he graduated at the latter in 1835. Returning to his home, he made a profession of his Christian faith, uniting with the Scotch Plains Baptist Church, under the pastorate of the Rev. John Rogers. In 1836 he settled, for the practice of the medical profession, in Newark, N. J., and united, by letter, with the First Baptist Church.

Those who knew him in early professional life can well recognize how, with his modesty, diffidence and reserve, he should thus far not have revealed the amount of knowledge he had acquired. Yet those who met him were impressed with his commanding personality, his urbane and quiet dignity, and somehow felt themselves in the presence of a superior nature.

Besides thorough preparation in his profession, he evidently had spent much of his time in the study of the classics, and had acquired an accurate knowledge thereof, such as is possessed by those only who have by dint of personal effort worked their way into the genius and technicalities of a dead language.

In 1842 he married Caroline E., a beautiful and accomplished daughter of Jonathan C., and Maria (Smith) Ackerman, of New Brunswick, N. J. She was very saintly and lovely in character, and much beloved by those who knew her. She died in 1847, leaving a son and a daughter who were thenceforth the only fond companions of his domestic circle. His great loss and his new responsibilities seem to have still more inclined him to devotion to his professional and scholastic studies.

In 1848 he went abroad, spending most of his time in hospitals, and in the society of the most eminent physicians and surgeons, of Europe. He was in Paris during the Revolution of June, 1848, which gave him special opportunities for surgical study.

When I entered his office, in 1849, he was regarded as the most accomplished practitioner of Newark, and as eminent both for his professional and literary acquirements. He had already found his practice sufficient to admit a partner, which he did all the more readily

because seeking to secure more time for literary study, and the indulgence of his taste both in art and literature. He had been favored in and out of his profession with such pecuniary success—resulting mostly from judicious investments in real estate—as enabled him to continue in practice chiefly for the love of his calling. He was fond of clinical exactness, was often called upon in consultation, especially in surgical cases, and had that conscientious regard for the welfare of his patients which led him carefully to study and observe, so as to be skillful in his treatment and devotedly attentive to those in his charge. In 1854, he again visited Europe. After an absence of seventeen months, during which he made the continental languages a study, he returned to his practice in Newark. He then devoted himself with increased knowledge and earnestness to professional work, and for many years, with another assistant, continued in the active practice of his profession.

In 1862, under the direction of an eminent English landscape gardener, he began the laying out and beautifying of seventeen acres of the ancestral farm at Scotch Plains, selecting for his plantings the choicest varieties of foreign and domestic trees, plants and shrubs. In one portion of this park, he located a reproduction of the famous labyrinth at Hampton Court, near London. In another part, he enclosed a large paddock for a herd of deer of his own raising. He built, subsequently, a house of brick and stone and native woods, in harmony with the grounds. In this he resided with his son and daughter, and was a most genial and entertaining host. His large library with its lofty roof was the special admiration of his many guests. Among the imported copies of antiques on the lawn is one of Æsculapius, and in the entrance hall of the mansion is Horatio Stone's marble bust of Harvey.

On the highest point of his mountain-land opposite his home, he erected a handsome rustic tower, two stories high, of which he makes mention in the following lines:

> The breezy summit of the neighboring Mount
> Blows bugle-summons, calling to the Muse
> To climb and meditate the prospect. Pulse
> Quickens, blood gallops in the veins, and throbs

The Young Hunters by A. Calandrelli (1874.)
Some of the Deer at Deerhurst.

> Impatient, knowing what awaits. O come!
> Delay not! Hasten! Leave the Plain, or lead
> Or follow! 'Gainst the steep opposing slope
> Plant eager feet, and, at each upward step,
> Look back to see how the horizon widens! High
> And higher yet keep climbing, till you reach
> The Tower above the tree-top lifted, so the eye
> Shall leap all barriers to the farthest blue!
> The Height is holy, and not far from God!

While retiring from the more active duties of a general practice, he was for many years daily at his Newark office; and also, as a favor, allowed many of those who lived near his country home, "Deerhurst," to avail themselves of his advice. In fact, it cannot be said that he relinquished practice at all, or allowed his increasing literary distinction and his business duties to interfere with his devotion to his chosen pursuit. He was eminently a physician, amid all other eminence. He delighted in his profession, both as a science and as an art. He felt his calling to be a sacred one. It was a part of his ministry for the Master whom he loved to serve. He lived to assuage pain, and to be courageous in relieving sickness and postponing death; rejoicing in the good he was thus enabled to do for humanity and for God.

How loyal he was to his profession, amid the greater glow of literary fame and the temptations of wealthy ease, let "The Microcosm" testify. This poetic address of his, as President of the Medical Society of New Jersey in 1866, should be read and re-read by every physician as an inspiration to accurate knowledge, to close analysis, to professional enthusiasm, and to adoring love. It leaves a poor excuse for any of us, if we are not inspired by the theme of our studies, and the object of our life service. It does not ignore that which is material and world-wise, but it crowns it with that which is spiritual and eternal. It shows how we have a mission to fulfill; and how integral and essential Christianity is to those who live to minister to their fellow-men in sickness and in death. As he expresses it in his note as to Vesalius: "The Divine Redeemer, the Incarnate Word, Maker of all things, Lord of life, is Lord also of the Sciences."

In the Physician's edition of "The Microcosm," as

published by the Appletons, he introduces several illustrations. One is the portrait of Vesalius devoutly engaged in dissection, which he inserts as illustrative of these lines:

> Dear God! this BODY, which, with wondrous art
> Thou hast contrived, and finished part by part,
> Itself a universe, a lesser all,
> The greater cosmos crowded in the small—
> I kneel before it, as a thing divine;
> For such as this, did actually enshrine
> Thy gracious Godhead once, when Thou didst make
> Thyself incarnate, for my sinful sake.
> Thou who hast done so very much for me,
> O let me do some humble thing for Thee!
> I would to every Organ give a tongue,
> That Thy high praises may be fitly sung:
> Appropriate ministries assign to each,
> The least make vocal, eloquent to teach.

Another is Rembrandt's well-known "Lesson in Anatomy," which he inserts with the description, beginning thus:

> The subject MUSCLES—girded to fulfill
> The lightning mandates of the sovereign Will—
> Th' abounding means of motion, wherein lurk
> Man's infinite capacity for work.

A third is "Harvey Demonstrating to Charles I, his Theory of the Circulation of the Blood":

> Make room, my HEART! that pour'st thyself abroad,
> Deep, central, awful mystery of God!

Well may he be called the Physician-Poet! He received the degree of A. M. from Rutgers College. In 1860 he received the degree of Ph.D. from Lewisburg University, and that of LL.D. from Princeton College in 1871.

Dr. Coles had reached such a vigorous old age as still to promise many years of life. In the early Spring (1891), he had the prevailing influenza, which left him with a cough, and some mild symptoms which puzzled him, as they have so many others, but which seemed to give no occasion for alarm. As a recreation, he proposed a trip to California with his son and daughter and a sister-in-law. They left home April 14th. The trip was a disappointing one, for, although his powerful constitution enabled him to go everywhere, his cough defied all treatment, and by reason thereof he grew weaker instead of stronger. After a week's stay at the beautiful Hotel del Monte, California, where he received every possible courtesy and attention, heart complication suddenly set in as a sequel to La Grippe. He was confined to his room but two days. Unable to recline, he calmly realized the serious nature of his symptoms. With great peace he bade adieu to his loved ones, reminded them to repeat, each morning, The Lord's Prayer, and to aid the objects dearest to his heart; then, with words of Christian faith and love, passed away, (May 3d, 1891), to be, as one of his own hymns so well expresses it—

   Ever, my Lord, with Thee,
    Ever with Thee!
   Through all eternity
    Thy face to see!
   I only ask to be
   Ever, my Lord, with Thee,
    Ever with Thee!

BIOGRAPHICAL SKETCH.

The funeral of Dr. Coles took place at the First Baptist Peddie Memorial Church, Newark, N. J., May 29th, and was largely attended by his medical and literary friends and those in other walks of life who had known him in the various relations he had sustained. The appropriate rendering of four of his hymns* added solemnity to the occasion, and emphasis to the many tributes to his earnest Christian life. His remains were interred in Willow Grove Cemetery, New Brunswick, N. J., beside those of his wife.

This notice would be incomplete without some fuller allusion to his literary labors, and to the marked traits of his character.

Soon after he settled in Newark, he became a contributor to the Newark Daily Advertiser, and early showed an interest in education, in a public library, in temperance movements, and in all objects looking to the welfare of society. Rarely attending any public meetings, he gave expression to his views in an occa-

---

*"Ever, My Lord, with Thee." Tune, *Bethany.*
"All the Days." Original music by W. F. Sherwin.
"Jesu Dulcis Memoria." Translation; tune, *Clifford.*
"Here are Partings and Painful Farewells." Tune, *Sweet By and By.*

sional address, and in the columns of the daily journals.

In poetry and prose, his literary taste and learning soon came to be recognized, and he had a local reputation long before he was more generally known.* It was, perhaps, his first translation of "Dies Iræ" (1847), that arrested the attention of linguists and scholars throughout the world. It was a difficult task to undertake, as there were several versifications of it by authors of classical note and learning. As he followed it, from time to time, with sixteen other versions, it was seen what opulence of resource was at his command.

Rev. Dr. Philip Schaff, in his recent work, "Literature and Poetry," referring to these, says, "A physician, Abraham Coles, has made (of the "Dies Iræ") seventeen versions in all, which show a rare fertility and versatility, and illustrate the possibilities of versification without altering the sense."

His translations of various other Latin hymns, as contained in his volume, "Latin Hymns with Original

---

* The catalogues of many of the libraries of Europe, especially those of Oxford and Cambridge, England, show the possession of one or more of the published works of Dr. Abraham Coles.

Translations," will ever be the admiration of scholars.*

"The Evangel" and "The Light of the World" give the Gospel story of our Lord in verse, with notes full of devotion and learning. His great love to Christ was his crowning excellence.†

John G. Whittier says: "Dr. Coles is a born hymn-writer. He has left us, as a legacy of inestimable worth, some of the sweetest of Christian hymns. His 'All the Days' and his 'Ever with Thee' are immortal songs. It is better to have written them than the stateliest of epics. No man living or dead has so rendered the *text* and the *spirit* of the old and wonderful Latin hymns."

---

* Dr. Coles has left, in manuscript, Translations of the whole of Bernard of Clairvaux's "Address to the Various Members of Christ's Body Hanging on the Cross," consisting of three hundred and seventy lines; the whole of Hildebert's "Address to the Three Persons of the Most Holy Trinity;" the first book of Vida's "Christiad;" several additional Latin hymns; selections from the Greek and Latin classics; and other writings in poetry and prose on literary, medical and scientific subjects.

† In his introduction to "The Evangel," Dr. Coles says: "The author has sought to cast down and tread under foot all egotisms, vanities and low ambitions; and if in his weakness and unworthiness he has done anything to make the adorable Redeemer the object of a warmer love and a firmer trust; to draw closer the bands of a common brotherhood in an undivided fellowship of Christian love; to make the Bible seem a dearer and a diviner book—its pages more luminous, its promises more precious, the heaven it reveals more certain—he would prize it infinitely more than the greatest epic success.

While these studies show his profound learning in the **Greek** and **Latin** languages, it is only when we look to the studies of his last years, in "A New Rendering of the Hebrew Psalms into English Verse," that we come to know of his knowledge of Oriental languages; of the vast realms of scholarship he had explored. But his stately and commanding prose has almost been obscured by his poetry. The marvel of all his books is in their introductions and notes. Whole folios of recondite learning are opened up in modest foot-notes, and the reader knows he is in company with one who has been delving and digging in the richest mines of unexplored knowledge. His sharp, quick sentences of introduction, and the grasp which he shows of his theme, are at once an admiration and a surprise.

His style has individuality as much as that of Dr. Johnson or of Thomas Carlyle. One constantly sees how thoughts sublime find expression in terse and stately sentences, and how words are chosen such as come out of the depths of inspiration and genius. There is not conformity to the style of any favorite author, or to the modes of thought of any formal logician, but a forging of weighty words, wrought out from the depths of great inner feelings and conceptions. Others will more fully analyze these mementoes of his greatness, but we, as physicians, may well linger in admiration, and rejoice that one of our own Society should have thus adorned a literature already rich in contributions from those educated in medical science, and proficient in medical art.

But the crown of all was his wonderful character. He did everything with conscientious precision and thoroughness; he was always after the depth of things. How he would sometimes work over the wording of a line, and then over a note that brought out its fullest meaning. So, too, he worked in his profession.

His respectful bearing toward all had its seat in a profound reverence. He was reverent of humanity because of his intense reverence for God and all his works. He studied nature and the Bible and the inner consciousness of the spiritual life with the same majestic, adoring insight. He was not religious by an effort. "I have," says Dr. Oliver Wendell Holmes, "always considered it a great privilege to enjoy the friendship of so pure and lofty a spirit; a man who seemed to breathe holiness as his native atmosphere, and to carry its influences into his daily life."

Had he not been poet, he would have been painter, or musical composer, because in no other way could his adoring enthusiasm have found symmetrical expression.

When he issued a book its typographical execution must be complete. He visited the great picture galleries of Europe, and at large expense selected the choicest specimens of ancient art to illustrate his themes. These gave expression to his character not less than to his taste.

When he wrote hymns it was because the inner music of his soul had to be set to metrical expression. He was a genius, but it was chiefly character and life that flowed out through his writings.

He became familiar with little children easier than with all others, because in them he saw more of nature, and more of faith, hope and charity.

He believed in his profession, because in it he realized the possibilities of high science and applied art for the uses of humanity, and so could be co-worker with the Great Physician, who went about doing good. We cherish his memory because we cherish skill, character, usefulness, and rejoice in having such a model. Such lives do not die, but live as incentives for those of all the ages. We cannot reach his fame, but we can imitate his devotion to knowledge, his reverence for life and goodness, his desire for usefulness, his holy faith, his humble affection for the good, the beautiful, the true.

MEMORIAL TRIBUTES.

IN MEMORIAM.

ABRAHAM COLES, M. D., LL. D., ENTERED INTO REST,
MAY 3, 1891.

This simple wreath upon his bier I lay—
This feeble tribute to his memory pay,
Not only for he was my father's friend,
And mine, steadfast and faithful to the end;
But day and night, to help his fellow men,
He wrought with skillful hands and able pen.
His wealth of ancient and of modern lore
He held in trust to serve the Master more;
In science versed, yet well did he uphold
The faith delivered to the saints of old;
The keen logician, hiding not his light,
With leveled lance he charged for truth and right.
The poet sweet, his graceful verses ran
In streams of love to God and love to man.

The course is finished now—fought the good fight;
Henceforth the victor's crown, the robe of white.
No more the gentle voice, the kindly face,
Shall welcome to the fair ancestral place,
Where Summer, matchless by the mountain side,
Holds queenly court; yet may our tears be dried,
For he the heaven-illumined path hath trod,
That leads unto the perfect peace of God.

THEOPHILUS BOND.

MEMORIAL TRIBUTES.

THE death of Dr. Coles, in California, was extensively noticed and commented upon by the press, religious and secular; and many letters of sympathy, mingled with expressions of respect and regard for the departed, were received by the members of his family.

On the second day after his death, the following editorial appeared in the "Newark Daily Advertiser:"

"The sudden death of Dr. Abraham Coles, which is announced in another column to-day, will cause a deep feeling of sadness, not only among the medical profession, of which he was a distinguished member, but especially in this community in which his active life was passed, and among the generation which loved and appreciated his rare virtues and sterling qualities of mind and heart. He sprang from fine old New Jersey stock, and inherited the literary, artistic and scientific tastes which he afterwards developed with conscientious and painstaking culture. He was a man of strong religious faith, positive political convictions, and inflexible purity of character. He had walked the hospitals of Paris, where he became an accomplished surgeon; and he practiced his profession with marked success. At the same time he devoted a large share of his energies to classical studies, and attracted the attention of literary men on both sides of the ocean by his careful translations of the famous old lyrics, the 'Dies Iræ' and 'Stabat Mater,' which were published in book form, with illustrations which he had selected from the best works of the old masters. He was also the author of many poems and reviews, and articles on various subjects of popular interest, some of which originally appeared in this paper. As one of the founders of the old Newark Library, and the Historical Society, and on account of his active efforts in the promotion of the religious, educational and scientific development of this city, his memory will be cherished with lasting affection and respect."

The "Union County Standard," after referring to the loss sustained by his native county by reason of his death, says:

"In his life Dr. Abraham Coles was sturdy in his convictions, and effective in carrying them out. He did much work for the right side in the abolition of slavery. His reverence for things eternal was as sincere as it was tolerant. He was an intimate and dear friend of George MacDonald, the English novelist. He maintained a friendly intimacy with John Bright, and with Oliver Wendell Holmes and John G. Whittier, and many other strong and good men. His deeds of kindness were as numerous as the hours he lived. He led a very beautiful life in his library, in communion with the departed and the living. His memory will always be pleasant as the memory of a friendly and just man made perfect."

From the "New York Tribune" we quote the following:

"Dr. Abraham Coles was widely known as a scholar, author and linguist. He was born at Scotch Plains, N. J., and spent the last years of his life there on his beautiful place, which was much resorted to by literary and professional people. For more than fifty years he pursued his literary studies and work, and became proficient in Greek, Latin, Hebrew, Sanskrit and the modern languages."

Report of the committee appointed by the President, George R. Kent, M. D., at a special meeting of the Essex County Medical Society, held May 11, 1891, to take action in regard to the death of Dr. Abraham Coles:

Mr. President and Gentlemen of the Society—

Your committee, appointed to draft resolutions upon the death of Dr. Abraham Coles, would respectfully report the following:

Whereas, This Society has learned, with profound regret of the death of Dr. Abraham Coles, for many years one of its most highly esteemed members, and at at one time its President; and,

Whereas, We desire to place upon record our sense of the loss we have thus sustained, as well as to testify our appreciation of his worth, be it

Resolved, That this Society recognizes, in the death of Dr. Coles, the loss of one possessed of those qualities which combine to make the true physician; dignified in manner, courteous, refined, painstaking, conscientious, with an innate gentleness of disposition, which caused him to shrink from the infliction of unnecessary pain, and with an affability which endeared him to those with whom he was brought into contact. He possessed, further, a skill, judgment and tact which caused him to be widely known to the profession, and which led to his aid and counsel being extensively sought after by his fellow practitioners.

He was an earnest man, positive in his convictions, with the courage to carry them out. In any step he undertook, he deliberated calmly, judged wisely and acted energetically. To this decision of character he owed his success in life, and much of the influence he exercised in the community where, as a citizen, he was respected and revered, and where his loss will be sadly felt.

In the Church, he was a sincere Christian, firm in his belief, and an ardent defender of his faith.

In the world of letters he attained enviable distinction, and we appreciate the honor thus conferred upon one of the members of our profession. Strongly imbued with literary tastes, and with mental endowments of a high order and a keen and analytical mind, he so improved his natural talents by close application and careful study as to gain for himself the esteem and friendship of the leading minds of the age.

But in his domestic and social relations the true character of the man showed itself to the best advantage. Those of us who had the pleasure of his friendship and hospitality can never forget his warm greeting, his solicitude for the enjoyment of all, without exception; his pleasant conversation and humor, his genial manner and his remarkable versatility, by which he could so readily adapt himself to a guest, whether child or philosopher.

As a friend, physician, citizen, author and Christian man, his death is a public loss.

Resolved, That we extend to his family our sincere sympathy in their bereavement, made the more painful by the circumstances under which his death occurred.

Resolved, That the Society attend his funeral as a body.

Resolved, That copies of these resolutions be furnished to his family, and also to the press, for publication.

Very respectfully,

ARTHUR WARD,
JOSEPH D. OSBORNE,
JOSEPH C. YOUNG.

The funeral services of Dr. Coles were held, May 29th, in Newark, N. J. The relatives, clergy and honorary pall-bearers, assembled in the Doctor's venerable brick and stone building on Market street, the home of his married life, and the birthplace of his children. After a short prayer by the Rev. Dr. A. H. Burlingham, the friends, in carriages, accompanied the body to the First Baptist Peddie Memorial Church, where the public services were held, the Rev. Dr. William W. Boyd, the pastor, presiding, and Prof. Edward M.

Bowman, the organist, taking charge of the music. In the account thereof, we quote from the "Daily Advertiser:"

"The building was filled with relatives and citizens, who had come to pay the last tribute of respect to the memory of Dr. Coles. The New Jersey Historical Society attended in a body. After the funeral march had been played, and the hymn, 'Ever With Thee,' sung, the Rev. Dr. A. H. Burlingham, of the Missionary Union, delivered an invocation. He was followed by Dr. Parks of the Scotch Plains Baptist Church, who read the seventeenth chapter of St. John, a special favorite of Dr. Coles. The Rev. Dr. Robert Lowry, of Plainfield, N. J., then offered the following prayer:

"'Our Lord, our Father, we bend before Thee. Thou art our Sovereign, our Father and our Friend. When it is dark we are not afraid, Thou art near us; even though we cannot see Thee, we turn our eyes towards Thee. Our hearts we lift up to Thee; we have consciousness of Thy presence. We do not need to look Thee in the face, we feel that Thou art near, and art here, more really seen by us than if Thou shouldst take our own form and present Thyself to our senses. Thou hast taught us this, so that anything that comes upon us in the succession of life's experiences need not appall us, for we can afford to wait until Thy finger shall trace everything before our eyes, and we shall see the present disorder resolving itself into forms of beauty because of Thy light. So it comes to pass we are not afraid of death. All its terrors are taken away, even though the flesh may sometimes shrink before them, the nerves sometimes quiver; even though some natural desire should spring up for the moment to stay a little longer with those whom we love upon the earth, yet we lay our hand of faith upon Thy promises, and we know that all things work together for the good of them that love God. We come to Thee now, not because we have need to tremble in Thy presence, but because Thou hast arrested us in our own highway of life that, we may turn aside for a moment, and think, think more spiritually, think more tenderly than we are wont to think, amid the hurry, and rush, and bustle, and dust of life.

"'We pray Thee, Lord, that Thou wouldst give unto us even at this hour, that seems to be dark, such revelation of Thyself as that we shall see light in the Lord, and the Lord shall shed His light all around us and we shall have no fear.

"'We thank Thee, Oh Thou blessed Providence, we thank Thee that the dropping of a tear sometimes is consistent with the highest degree of joy, that Thou dost Thyself, as it would seem to us, look upon the very tears that fall from our eyes and, behold, our faces take the kindling of Thy love. Oh, give us that shining now! We have had, some of us, long years of friendship, companionship and comradeship with Thy servant. We have walked with him; we have talked with him; we have been with him in his silence; we have listened to what he has said; we have taken his counsel; we have looked upon his life; we have gazed upon his quiet face as it presented itself before us; we have looked at the hair which was whitening upon his head; we have caught sometimes something of the sweet, precious spirit that animated him; and we have felt at such times as if the world was better because he was in it, and we were better because we were near him. It is a sweet memory we have to-day. We should be base in our own eyes if we did not rejoice that we had such a memory; and as we call up the form that became so familiar to us with its dignity, with its charm, with the very sweetness with which it passed before us, we place a reverence on the man; and it is a glorious memory to us that we knew him, and were in the circle of his friendship, and could feel his touch, and get something of his blessed inspiration.

"'Lord, we thank Thee that he came in our day and generation, a man laden with such wealth; with such wealth of character; with such wealth of talent; such blessed power to catch Thy thought and translate it, and send it out to those who might get that thought through him. We thank Thee for the blessed lines he wrote, quivering with poetic spirit, blazing with poetic fire, setting us aflame sometimes when we read them. We thank Thee for his strong principles, for the integrity of his character, the richness of his life.

"'Oh, how good Thou art to Thy people, good in Thy gifts, good in Thy marked bestowance, good in Thy generous providences; but, against the background of Thy general goodness, comes out this one man, and we look at him and admire him; we get close to him, we bend our ear to him, and try to catch what he says; we strive to imbibe the very spirit with which he was filled. As a great circle of friends, we are called upon to thank Thee; as a great band of religionists, we are called upon to thank Thee; as a great community, we do thank Thee, and we pray Thee now that Thou wouldst graciously come to these dear ones whom Thou hast left to us. Their hearts are down low to-day, when they look earthward and they think of their desolate home; when they think of the places which must always now be vacant; when they think of the books that he touched, and they touched with him, and the words that he read to them, and to which they listened; the voice now never to sound in their ears again, never to send its thrill upon the strings of their hearts. We pray for them. Be Thou their comfort. We pray that Thou wouldst go before them as they return to their habitation, and meet them at the door, and bid them welcome; welcome to a place filled with Thyself, and with the best and sweetest memories that children can have of a parent.

" 'Lord, hear and graciously guide; and, when flesh and heart fail, receive us, also, to be with Thee amid Thy glory, through Jesus Christ, our Lord. Amen.'

"Here followed the singing of Dr. Coles' hymn, 'All the Days,' by Mr. James Sauvage, and a chorus of selected voices, accompanied by the organ.

"The Rev. Charles F. Deems, D. D., LL. D., of New York, paid a tender tribute to Dr. Coles' high social, intellectual and spiritual characteristics. He said:

" 'A special honor has been put upon me by the family in asking me to take part in these services of respectful memory to a man whose name will not soon be let die. I come as the President of the American Institute of Christian Philosophy, of which he was a member, and to whose proceedings he made contributions, which will be preserved many a year, and which have been read, as I know, in Europe and America with very great satisfaction, by men who are devoting themselves to thinking along the lines of Christian investigation.

" 'I had a friend once, a bishop, a very great man, who said : " I would give all I have ever had in my possession, of surroundings, of influence and of position, to be the author of one hymn." Well he might. To be the author of one hymn that is sung a hundred years after a man's death, is better than to have been an emperor. Dr. Coles was that. With his rare combination of talents, this man would have been the distinguished poet he was if he had devoted himself only to the art of poetry; with his very rare combination of talents this man would have been distinguished in regions of science had he devoted himself simply to science. But he combined them all so as to make a rounded and beautiful character; and there was such a sweetness and charm about the man that wherever he went he made friends.

" 'My first acquaintance with him was through the study of Latin hymns. I hunted up his works, and I found that a great many men were better acquainted with his reputation than I was; and then I thought that I would like to see Abraham Coles, and when I did see him he was such a winsome man, he was so charming, that in five minutes after I first met him I felt that somehow I must have long been a very intimate friend, such was the nature of his character.

" 'There is a man lying there whose fingers touched the chords that brought responses from hearts in every portion of the Christian Church and of the reading world, moving old and young, heretic and orthodox. Here amongst his brethren, his intimates and children, in the name of all that is true in Christianity; in the name of all that is worth living in life, of all that is worth having in death, of all that is worth gathering in eternity; in the name of the Holy Catholic Church of God; in the name of all Christian people upon the face of the earth; in the name of all these many chords that he has touched, and that are making response all over the world to-day—I stand and make my salutations to my venerable brother as he ascends to his coronation: Hail, brother, hail and farewell!'

"The Rev. Dr. Boyd, at the conclusion of Dr. Deems' address, read a number of letters from Protestant and Catholic clergymen, and others, paying high tribute to Dr. Coles' worth, expressing sympathy for the family on account of the bereavement, and regrets at inability to be present at the funeral services.

"'I think,' continued Dr. Boyd, 'Dr. Coles, in the spirit of his life—for you know he was a great admirer of Mr. Lincoln*—came as near as any one I ever knew to fulfilling the maxim, "With malice towards none, with charity towards all." It is very beautiful to see how times of sorrow bring us all into one communion of Christian feeling and affection, no matter how widely we may be separated in our religious beliefs; it is a foretaste of the unity which is beyond.

* During the war, Dr. Coles wrote the following sonnet, now first published:

> Lincoln! twice summoned to the helm of state,
> Be thine to bring a calm upon the deep.
> In which the eyes of war may ever sleep!
> Quell bloody enmity and civil hate!
> From all unchristian broils and homicides,
> By the religious sword of Justice, free
> The land baptized anew to liberty!
> Search out where unrepentant Treason hides—
> Thy soul's eye sharpened with that sacred Light
> Of whom the sun itself is but a beam;
> And be thou firm and faithful to the Right.
> Though topt with titles, high in men's esteem,
> To Virtue's pilotage must thou resort,
> Else shipwreck shall betide in safest port.

" 'It now gives me great pleasure to introduce to you as a representative of our denomination, Rev. Dr. Boardman, of Philadelphia, in whose life and spirit we have a most beautiful example of this sentiment of Christian unity.'

"The Rev. George Dana Boardman then made the concluding address. He said:

" 'I do not wonder that our revered friend was so fond of the chapter which has been read. This chapter, as we all know, is the Holy of holies in the tabernacle of the Most High. How beautiful to know that the last night our Lord was upon earth as a suffering man, He, first of all, prayed for Himself, even though He was the Apostle and High Priest of our profession. Yet there is no tinge of weakness in this prayer. It is hardly a prayer. It is the request which a co-equal may present to his co-equal. Next, He prays for those who had steadfastly continued with Him in His temptation. How beautiful to think that He prayed for those chosen Eleven, who, it may be, were still standing or kneeling with Him in that room where He had gathered the representatives of His infant church. Lastly, He prayed for His church universal through all coming time. How comforting to know that, having prayed for Himself and His Apostles, the Son of Man, with that strange prescience, that blessed foresight, which became Him as the Son of God, thought of you and me, praying for you, beloved children of our noble friend; for you, his mourning relatives; you, members of the church to which he belonged and to which he was so faithful; even those of you who were associated with him in professional and in municipal ties, and for aught I know in ties even more sacred; and for you, members of that great Church of the Saints who call upon the name of our Lord Jesus Christ in every place, "their Lord and ours!"

"'I entirely agree with what my esteemed friend, Dr. Deems, has said this afternoon. When a man of God dies and is taken to his home, it is a time for hosannahs. Christ has preceded us into glory, and with our honored and loved friend from New York we may truly say, to-day is the day of triumph.

"'This is a touching memorial service which we have had this afternoon. Here is my friend from New York, of another spiritual communion; here is a letter representing the largest church upon the face of the earth, and holding within its embrace thousands of the Lord's elect ones; and here, too, is a letter from one whom, so far as I know, belongs to no earthly Christian church bearing any particular denominational name—all gathered together to do honor and tribute to the memory of a man of God. The secret of this is found in that prayer which was read to-day, "Neither pray I for these alone, but for them also which shall believe on me through their word." In these days of ecclesiastical tumult and confusion, of hurrying to and fro, it is pleasant to feel that we are moored in apostolic harbors, or rather, in Christ's own Haven, "that they all may be one, as thou, Father, art in me, and I in thee, that they also may be one in us: that the world may believe that thou hast sent me." It is Jesus Christ who is the bond of union; it is Jesus Christ who is the germinal principle of the harvest which shall come to the church of Jesus Christ.

"'I am not here to pronounce a eulogy on our friend. I have no doubt that in due time there will be the elaborate and proper tribute to the upright citizen, to the public-spirited patriot, to the skillful physician, to the erudite scholar, to the devout poet, to the Christian philanthropist. Meantime it is for you and for me to join in that magnificent, triumphant retinue that are following the Lord of the Worlds into the rest which remains for the people of God.'

"Here followed the singing of Dr. Coles' translation of St. Bernard's hymn, 'Jesu Dulcis Memoria.'

"Dr. Boyd said :

"'We have received a very beautiful tribute to Dr. Coles from the pen of the Rev. Dr. McArthur, of New York, but as the hour is getting late, and these friends must go to the place of interment, I shall omit reading it, and we may hope to see it in print.

"'As the casket is borne from the church after the closing prayer, may I ask that the audience remain, and may I ask the choir to sing at the close of the prayer, these words of Dr. Coles:

"'Here are partings and painful farewells,
And the sunderings of tenderest ties;
In that heavenly land where He dwells
God shall wipe away tears from all eyes.

In the Sweet By and By,
We shall meet on that beautiful shore.

"Here the pilgrim can scarcely discern
The reward for the tears that he sheds.
But the ransomed with joy shall return
With perpetual joy on their heads.

"Let us pray.

"'Almighty and most merciful Father, who hath given us grace at this time with one accord to make our common supplications unto Thee, and dost promise that when two or three are gathered together in Thy name, Thou wilt grant their request, fulfill now, we pray Thee, the desires and petitions of Thy servants, as may be most expedient for us, granting us in this world the knowledge of Thy truth, and in the world to come, life everlasting. Amen.

"'And now may the grace of our Lord Jesus Christ, the love of God, and the communion of the Holy Ghost, be with you all. Amen.'

"As the casket was being borne from the church, the choir sang as requested, after which the body, accompanied by the Rev. Dr. Boyd and the relatives, was taken to Willow Grove Cemetery, New Brunswick, and placed beside that of his wife.

"The following gentlemen acted as honorary pall-bearers: Vice Chancellor Abraham V. Van Fleet, Judge David A. Depue, ex-Chancellor Theodore Runyon, Hon. Amzi Dodd, Hon. Thomas N. McCarter, Hon. Cortlandt Parker, Hon. A. Q. Keasbey, Hon. F. W. Ricord, Alexander H. Ritchie, William Rankin, Charles Kyte, Noah Brooks, Edmund C. Stedman, Wilson Schoch, Spencer Goble, Dr. S. H. Pennington, Dr. A. W. Rogers, Dr. Ezra M. Hunt, Dr. B. L. Dodd, Dr. J. C. Young and Dr. T. H. Tomlinson."

The Rev. Dr. Robert S. MacArthur, of New York, was invited to take part in the services. On account of illness, he was unable to attend. In a letter he wrote as follows :

"Perhaps the words that I enclose might be read as expressive of my appreciation of Dr. Coles' poetical genius, medical attainments and Christian character.

"Few men have recently died whose position and work were so unique as those of Dr. Abraham Coles. Seldom are so many elements of power united in a single man. His death caused genuine sorrow to wide and influential circles of appreciative friends. He was a distinguished member of the medical profession, having given to it years of devoted study and earnest labor in its practical duties. His poetical genius was as rare as it was genuine. There is no kind of literary fame so enduring as the authorship of a noble hymn. As the author of the hymn beginning, 'From Thee Begetting Sure Conviction,' his name will live, even as he has described the presence of the Master as continuing with His people, 'All the Days. All the Days.' We sang that hymn in the Calvary Church when we first entered our new church home. We sing it on many of our anniversary occasions. Other hymns which he has written are doubtless equally as good, but this one has for me a peculiar charm.

"Many of his translations of the Psalms are worthy to perpetuate his name to remote generations. I love to read them aloud that I may get the full force of their rhythm, as well as the sweet influence of their divine thought. His knowledge of general literature and especially of Latin hymnology gives him a special place in the thought and affection of students of the early days of the Christian Church. But most of all, his beautiful character as father, friend, neighbor, citizen and Christian man is worthy of the greatest emphasis on this occasion.

"I might fill page after page in expansion of this thought. He has graduated from earth, and matriculated into a higher school of science, of poetry, of literature, of art and of character—in the Celestial University, with the Lord Jesus as his instructor. With a depth of meaning which we never before appreciated can we now read, with fresh interest, his hymn which he loved on earth, and whose meaning he now understands as never before :

>"'Ever, my Lord, with Thee,
>   Ever with Thee !
> Through all eternity,
>   Thy face to see !
> I count this heaven, to be
> Ever, my Lord, with Thee,
>   Ever with Thee !'"

The Rev. Dr. Theodore L. Cuyler, being also prevented from attending the funeral services, wrote as follows:

"BROOKLYN, May 28th, 1891.

"I wish I could be present and offer my humble and heartfelt tribute to the spiritually-minded Christian, the cultured scholar and the zealous reformer, who was so widely known and loved.

"My first knowledge of Dr. Abraham Coles was from a tribute once paid to him by the brilliant and erudite Rev. Dr. Wm. R. Williams, of New York. It was a well-deserved commendation of his fine rendering of the 'Dies Iræ.' When I have given out from my pulpit Dr. Coles' beautiful hymn, 'All the Days,' I have told my congregation something about the noble man who composed it. How well I now recall his fine, handsome, benignant face; and his courteous manners and instructive conversation. He is now up among the singers of the 'new song,' and wears his well-won crown."

The Rev. Dr. Philip Schaff, Honorary Corresponding Secretary of the Evangelical Alliance of the United States, was invited to preach the funeral sermon; being absent, however, in Jacksonville, Illinois, he was unable to be present. In a letter to the family, he wrote:

"Could I by any possibility have attended the funeral of your venerable father, I would have done so and performed the sad and solemn duty of preaching the funeral sermon, as you wished me to do. As it is, I can only express my sincere condolence and to thank you for the honor you have done me by your request. Your good father has enjoyed a green old age, and left you the precious legacy of a spotless character and useful life, beautified by the charm of sacred poetry and song. I had known his translations of Latin hymns for many years before I had the pleasure of making his personal acquaintance on that memorable visit to your delightful home."

The following was received from the Rev. Richard S. Storrs, D. D., LL. D., of Brooklyn:

"BROOKLYN, N. Y., May 28th, 1891.

"Dr. Storrs regrets his inability to attend the funeral services of Dr. Abraham Coles, for whom he had a sincere and high regard, on account of other appointments for Friday, the 29th inst. He is grateful for the courtesy which numbers him among those to whom notice of the services was sent."

James Russell Lowell, between whom and Dr. Coles there existed a sincere and affectionate admiration, wrote as follows:

"ELMWOOD, CAMBRIDGE, May 28th, 1891.

"I regret very much that I cannot share in the sad function (that of pall-bearer), with an invitation to which I have been honored by the family of the late Dr. Coles. But my health will not permit it."

The above was one of the latest notes penned by the distinguished "poet and patriot."

Mrs. Mabel Lowell Burnett, daughter of James Russell Lowell, wrote from Elmwood, Cambridge, to the daughter of Dr. Coles:

"My father has been for some time so ill that he has not been able to write any letters. * * * I think it better to write myself to tell you of his illness, as a reason for his not giving you the sympathy which he would feel for you in your deep sorrow."

William Dean Howells wrote as follows to the family of Dr. Coles:

"BOSTON, May 29th, 1891.

"Your letter offering me the privilege of acting as pall-bearer at your father's funeral reached me duly to-day. You will believe that I was touched and honored by your thought of me, and I am sorry that I could not respond by my presence at the sad occasion. I need not praise your father to you, or try to tell you how much you have lost. All who ever saw his benign face must share your loss, but you alone know how great it is. My wife joins me in cordial sympathy."

In reply to a request to act as one of the pall-bearers at the memorial service, Justice Bradley, of the United States Supreme Court, wrote as follows:

"WASHINGTON, D. C., May 29th, 1891.

"I was very sorry that I could not comply with your wish that I should act as one of the pall-bearers of your father. He was one of my warmest friends, for whom I had not only the highest esteem, but affectionate friendship. We walked side by side in the path of life for more than half a century, with the warmest mutual regard. I have been separated lately somewhat by official duties here, but it has never interrupted our friendship.

"I tender you my sincerest sympathies for the loss of so excellent a father, and beg to express my own heartfelt sorrow for the breaking of another link that connected me with many past associations and happy recollections."

Alexander Hay Ritchie, artist and engraver, one of "Scotia's Sons," a "friend of the poet, tried and leal," wrote :

"Sorrowfully and humbly I accept the honor the family of Dr. Abraham Coles has done me, by their kind invitation to act as pall-bearer of their honored father."

Samuel H. Pennington, M. D., says :

"You do not overestimate the warm affection I had for my friend, your honored and beloved father, whose decease I sincerely deplore. It will afford me melancholy satisfaction to render the service to which you kindly invite me."

Hon. A. Q. Keasbey wrote :

"I esteem it a privilege to be allowed to testify my sympathy for you, and my regard for the memory of my old friend, by sharing in the final tribute on Friday."

Alexander W. Rogers, M. D., a venerable and distinguished physician, of Paterson, N. J., from early boyhood an intimate and cordial friend of Dr. Coles, writes :

"I hardly know what to say, or how to think, of my changed relations to my dear friend, your father. He is not dead, nor does he sleep. That mind, which was always so active in thinking about the great, and high, and blessed things, which pertained to life and godliness, and how to make his fellow mortals have better and higher aspirations—so active that he took less natural sleep than others—does not lie dormant. True, in one sense, he 'sleeps in Jesus'; he has that 'blessed sleep,' which is rest from all labor and toil. He thinks, and soars aloft in contemplation, without effort or fatigue; no longer any painful, tiresome research in old books, or new, for true ideas; or labored trial for the most proper expression of accumulated lore. He now knows as he is known, and has an angel tongue; and, more than when here, I believe, he can voice the adoration of his God, and chant the glory of his Redeemer. I think of him as gone on a journey, or, for a residence in a happier clime, where we hope to meet him by and by. While we have the same, or more, tender regard for him that we have always had, we know that he has the same for us; and being so much nearer to our great Friend, from whom we receive all that is good, will he not remember us, and our highest needs? We give, or offer up, no prayer for the dead—they are beyond our help, beyond any need from us—but may they not aid us? It is certain that their presence, in the better land, should be a stimulative to all our higher aspirations, that we may be prepared to join them there."

Noah Brooks, "Castine," author, editor of the Newark "Daily Advertiser," etc., wrote:

"I reply at once to your request to act as one of the pall-bearers at the funeral of your lamented father. If it will give you any satisfaction to have me take this melancholy duty, you may be sure I will do it. With sympathy for you in your great loss, I am, yours truly."

The Rt. Rev. Michael A. Corrigan, Catholic Archbishop of New York, in addition to words appreciatory of Dr. Coles as a translator of Latin hymns, says :

"I remember your good father with great respect, and will always cherish his memory with reverence. He was a good neighbor and a kind friend."

J. Marron Dundas, of Philadelphia, Pa., writes :

"Word has just reached me of the death of your honored father, Dr. A. Coles. As a lover of classical literature and an unworthy member of that church which gave birth to the 'Dies Iræ,' permit me, though a stranger, to sympathize with yourself and family in your great sorrow. All lovers of learning will feel his loss. All Catholics who knew the man or his works will murmur with my humble self, *requiescat in pace*."

The Hon. John Wanamaker, Postmaster General, sent the following from Washington, D. C.:

"I sympathize with you most truly in the sorrow that has come upon you."

The poet Whittier writes from Amesbury, Mass., June 3d, 1891:

"Illness has prevented me from writing some word expressing my sympathy with the many who mourn the death of a great and good man, who has left us a legacy of inestimable worth, some of the sweetest of Christian hymns. His 'All the Days' and his 'Ever With Thee' are immortal songs. It is better to have written them than the stateliest of epics. With him it is well. Thy aged friend,

"JOHN G. WHITTIER."

Dr. Oliver Wendell Holmes writes as follows:

"BOSTON, June 9th, 1891.

"I should reproach myself for not having written to you before this had not my time been taken up with cares and griefs which gave me so much to think of that I could claim forgiveness for many omissions which seemed like negligence. * * * * The death of your father puts out another light in the fast-gathering evening shadows. I have always considered it a great privilege to enjoy the friendship of so pure and lofty a spirit—a man who seemed to breathe holiness as his native atmosphere, and to carry its influences into his daily life. What precious memories you have to carry with you all your life; not only that there was no line which dying he could have wished to blot, but that there was no line which the purest of God's angels, looking over his shoulder, would not have looked upon approvingly.

"It is a blessed record your father has left. His memory will long be cherished as one of our truest and sweetest singers; and the most precious of consolations, now that he is not with you in bodily presence, is in remembering all that he has been."

Mrs. Benjamin Harrison, the wife of the President of the United States of America, wrote to the daughter of Dr. Coles as follows:

"EXECUTIVE MANSION, WASHINGTON, D. C.

"I was very much surprised and learned with much sorrow of the death of your father. From what you said, I presumed he was not well, but had no idea the end was so near. Death, however, often takes our friends when we least expect it. You have my warmest sympathy in your desolation and sorrow; but you also have the consolation of knowing that his wish is realized, 'Ever, My Lord, With Thee.'"

Julia Ward Howe writes:

"I heard of the death (of Doctor Abraham Coles) with sincere regret. The good Doctor had always been most kind to me and mine. * * * * The public recognition of his merits as a poet and as a man of letters will not fill the void he has left."

Florence Howe Hall, a daughter of Julia Ward Howe, and a resident of Scotch Plains, contributed to one of the leading journals the following testimonial:

"There have been numerous tributes to the worth and nobility of character, the scholarly tastes and attainments, of Dr. Abraham Coles, 'poet, man of letters and physician.' Among the 'wreaths of laurel and holly' there is still perhaps room for a plain 'spray of Western pine'—and I fain would say a few words of him, as I knew him—as kind friend and neighbor, as a gentleman whose courtesy of manner was only equalled by its simplicity, and above all, as 'the good physician'—the man whose mission it was to save life, to battle with and conquer disease. How nobly he fulfilled his duties as a high priest of the great art of healing, hundreds, perhaps thousands, know—his colleagues, above all, his grateful patients, know.

"In time of trouble he was a tower of strength. If a beloved child fell ill, we felt safe when the 'old Doctor' (as he was affectionately called) crossed the threshold—and in his green old age there yet abode the power and wisdom to save and heal, as his revered Master was wont to save and heal. Ever watchful, ever alert, anxious with the anxiety born of wide knowledge and long experience, yet brave and firm as became a man of undaunted courage and well-proved skill, he met the enemy—disease—at every point, and through the long struggle his assiduity never flagged, his resource never failed him. As I look back upon a certain hideous winter, when I lay on a bed of pain, prostrated by a fever that would not yield, I feel that to him I owe a debt of gratitude that can never be paid—I owe him my life! Although Dr. Coles was at this time seventy-three years of age, and the winter was a very severe one, the weather stormy, the ground covered with ice and snow, this kind physician and true friend came to see me twice a day, through cold and wind and storm. Sometimes I would beg him not to expose himself in such inclement weather, but he refused to spare himself—he felt that his duty was to his patient.

"A little boy, a son of a neighbor of ours, lay dying of diphtheria some years ago. The physician in attendance gave up all hope, but the father of the child asked leave to call Dr. Coles in consultation. He came and saw that heroic measures alone could save the little life. With those wonderfully skillful fingers of his, he performed the necessary operations on the poor little throat—his courage and calmness did not fail him in the crisis—the child is alive and well to-day!

"A friend, whose face was stained with weeping, said to me, at this good man's funeral, 'I always have thought my D—, my darling child, would have lived if Dr. Coles could have been with him.' This was the universal feeling among the patients—perfect faith in him who 'kept the faith' so nobly. His tenderness with little children made them all willing to come to him, and his wonderful skill as a nurse enabled many a weary mother to arrange bandages and persuade the child to swallow unpleasant potions, in spite of the latter's decided aversion to doing so. A beautiful friendship subsisted between him and a little girl of three or four years of age, who always spoke of him as 'her dear Doctor.' When her parents moved away from Scotch Plains, the little one was well nigh inconsolable at the separation. She talked much and often of her dear old friend—longed to see him again, and kept, among her most treasured possessions, a sweet little poem which he addressed to her.

"A man of unfailing courtesy, the modesty and simplicity of his demeanor were so great that he seemed like one receiving favors, where he was really conferring them. It was a pleasure to visit him in his beautiful library, surrounded by the books that he so dearly loved. He always had some new or interesting book to show, and when the visit was over, he insisted upon accompanying his visitors not only to the door of his house, but to the gateway of his beautiful place. We would remonstrate, but in vain, and he sometimes would make this little pilgrimage bareheaded; bare, that is, save for the noble fleece of silver-white hair that crowned his fine, massive head.

"Although so much of his time, during the latter years of his life, was spent in his study and by his own fireside, Dr. Coles was of a social nature, and seemed thoroughly to enjoy the reunions when we had the pleasure and privilege of being entertained beneath his roof, or of meeting him at the houses of his friends. His fine mind and genial disposition made him very agreeable in conversation, and he was an attentive listener as well as a good converser. As might have been expected in one whose mental faculties were so alert and active, he had a keen sense of humor. He thoroughly appreciated a good story, and no touch of satire, however delicate, was fine enough to escape his instant comprehension. The responsive twinkle of merriment in those bright gray eyes, the quiver of the sensitive mouth, and often a little quiet, half-suppressed laughter, showed his appreciation of jest or *bon mot*. Though a man of deep religious feeling, and one who thought much about the inner and the future life, Dr. Coles was also a man of the world, in the good sense of those words. His experience of men and affairs had been large and wide, and lifted him far above the petty spirit which can understand and appreciate only a narrow range of men and ideas.

"His dominant and eminent personality is so indissolubly associated in our minds with the beautiful grounds and noble trees whose shade was so dear to him, that it is difficult to conceive of his home apart from himself. Though we shall not again see his earthly form wandering among the familiar paths of 'Deerhurst,'

we shall always lovingly associate him with those acres whose beauty he created, with those trees which grew up under his watchful care.

"His fine, strong, yet tender, spirit has left us for the world of which he loved to think. We miss him sadly from his accustomed places—his loss throws a shadow on the beauty of the spring. But we rejoice that he lived among us, that here he fought the good fight, and left us a shining example of the faithful performance of duty which we would strive to emulate!"

Mrs. Julia Parmly Billings, (widow of Hon. Frederick Billings), prominent in good works, writes to the daughter of Dr. Coles from Woodstock, Vermont:

"Let me assure you of my deep sympathy in the loss, which must leave your home sad and lonely. For your father, 'the good physician' and noble man, I felt the greatest esteem. My children, also, mourn for their father, for this is their first summer without him. May the same precious faith that sustained them both be your heritage."

The Hon. Cortlandt Parker, LL. D., in his letter of acceptance, wrote:

"Of course I will be one of the pall-bearers at your father's funeral. It will be a sorrowful satisfaction to me. Your father was a very old friend of mine. I think he was a student of medicine when I was in the law office of my preceptor. If not, he had only just begun his practice. Judge Joseph P. Bradley, Mr. Frederick

Theodore Frelinghuysen and myself resuscitated an almost dead literary and debating society, and among its earliest members was your father. He was an earnest and painstaking member. He was distinguished from the beginning in composition. I remember his essays well. I remember his fervid piety, manly, outspoken, yet humble and unpretentious, then as always. We became warm friends. It is a pride, with me, that we always remained such.

"Your father's character seems to me to have been made up of three things—humility, sense of duty and manliness. What his hand found to do, he did with his might, and he never held back from the avowal or support of his opinions. His self-education was constant. Not a day, as I think, but he was busy, going forward in his own way intellectually. And his success all know. You say little when you say that he was fully prepared for the change. A firmer, humbler, more sincere believer in his Saviour and the salvation He died to give us never lived.

"He is a great loss—though he lived so long, and his death was to be expected, when it came it was a shock to all who knew him. The world goes on, unconscious of its losses. But they are losses, nevertheless."

Rev. Robert Lowry, D. D., of Plainfield, N. J., writes:

"It was a great privilege for me to be present at the services in Newark. Under any circumstances, I would have found a way of contributing the testimony of my presence to the exalted worth of the citizen and friend who had so sadly been taken from us. To have an actual participation in the last solemn rites was indeed a great though sorrowful satisfaction. I felt as though I wanted to lift up my voice before that gathering of sincere mourners, and tell them how this man had impressed himself on my life, and what lofty conceptions of intellectual and Christian life had been stirred within me in personal contact with him. It was a sweet and sad occasion to me, and I realized how much one man was worth to his fellow-men."

Dr. Coles, on his fifty-eighth birthday (December 26th, 1871), was agreeably surprised to receive from the Rev. James McCosh, D. D., LL. D., then President of Princeton College, the following communication:

"PRINCETON, N. J., Dec. 23d, 1871.
"DR. ABRAHAM COLES:

"Dear Sir—I have great pleasure in intimating that the Board of Trustees of the College of New Jersey, did on the 20th inst. confer on you the honorary degree of LL. D., to mark their appreciation of your literary ability."

On June 5th, 1891, Dr. McCosh wrote to the family of Dr. Coles:

"I had great respect and affection for your father. His poetry was of so lofty a type that he deserved the honorary degree (LL. D.) conferred upon him. * * * He has set you a fine example. I feel much for you under your sad privation. I myself must soon follow those who have gone before."

Richard W. Gilder writes as follows:

"Editorial Department, the Century Magazine,
"UNION SQUARE, New York.

"Illness prevented my writing to you at the time of your father's death, but I cannot refrain from still saying a word to you of appreciation of his character and talent, and of his personal kindness to me when I was a youth in Newark. He was one of the true men of this world—a good friend, a good citizen, a poet, a man. His personal presence was remarkable—a mingling of sweetness and dignity. He felt with the crowd, with the masses of humanity; but lived in an atmosphere to which few of them could attain—high above them. I have seldom met such a character. The world is poorer in his loss, though still holding in many ways the product of his refined nature and upright example."

Rev. Wayland Hoyt, D. D., writes from Minneapolis, Minnesota:

"A good, true and endearing life has gone to its crowning. * * * * I am, most sincerely yours."

"The Critic" (N. Y.), in its issues of May 9th and June 20th, says:

"There was no more scholarly man in New Jersey than Dr. Abraham Coles, who was best known for his translations of the 'Dies Iræ.' Although he practiced medicine in Newark, he made his home at Scotch Plains, N. J. The name of his place, 'Deerhurst,' was given to it because of its deer park, in which the owner kept a

fine herd of these beautiful animals. Dr. Coles' library or study at Deerhurst was an ideal room, not only on account of the scholar's library it contained, but because of its architectural attractions, the plentiful light coming from the top, its inviting fire-place and its easy chairs. Dr. Coles was devoted to his home, and nothing delighted him more than to entertain his friends there. I well remember one afternoon some fifteen years ago, when a party of ten of us drove over from Newark and stopped to pay our respects, Dr. Coles being our family physician at the time. Although we were unexpected guests, neither Dr. Coles nor his daughter would listen to our returning home until we had had our supper. If preparations had been making for a week, we could not have had a more bountiful or better served meal, nor a better time; but that goes without saying, for Dr. Coles was as delightful as a host as he was gifted as a poet."

Frederick W. Ricord, author and poet, Librarian of the New Jersey Historical Society, etc., wrote:

"For your dear father I cherished the tender affection of a brother. To him in my early life I hesitated not to go for aid and counsel, and with a brother's solicitude, he always welcomed me with open arms. You may be sure that the announcement of his departure gave me a pang such as the heart receives but seldom during even a lengthened lifetime. * * * * I ask for no more blissful heaven than that to which your dearly beloved father has gone."

The Rev. Wendell Prime, D. D., editor of the "New York Observer," writes from "Bonnie Corner," Hawthorne avenue, Yonkers, N. Y.:

"Again and again, I am led to think of your beloved and gifted father, and the sorrow that such a life leaves, with its brightness added to the heavenly glory. Ere long the same grace shall make it ours also."

Mary J. Porter, associate editor of the "Christian Intelligencer," writes from Bridgewater, Mass.:

"The daily papers bring the sad news of your great loss. * * * I shall always be glad that I had the pleasure of being in Dr. Coles' society. He was so stately in presence, so calm in action, so considerate of the happiness of others, that one recognized in him at once a prince among men."

Rev. Edward P. Terhune, D. D., of Brooklyn, N. Y., writing for himself and in behalf of his accomplished wife, "Marion Harland," says:

"When the announcement of the death of your dear father appeared, both Mrs. Terhune and myself were greatly shocked. For the many years of our residence in Newark, N. J., he was a frequent visitor at our home, always bringing to us his own genial spirit and cheer, and was welcome as one of our best friends. Since our removal, we had cherished the remembrance of those days; but our occasional reunions always gladdened us and left the pleasant savor of those earlier ties.

"Our sympathy with you is most hearty. I desire to bear my testimony to the nobility of your father's character, to his combined strength and gentleness, as well as to his marked talent and scholarship. We had been associated in circumstances that heightened my appreciation of him both as the man and the Christian."

The Rev. George M. Van Derlip, a member of the Century Club, surprised Dr. Coles, in July, 1890, at Deerhurst, with a gift, bearing the inscription, "To Abraham Coles, M. D., LL. D., Scholar and Poet, with the respects of the Century Association, New York." After the Doctor's death, he wrote:

"CENTURY CLUB, 7 West 43d St., NEW YORK.

"I feel the loss of your father to be a personal deprivation as well as grief. I was very glad I could arrange to be at the funeral. I have seldom, almost never, seen such an array of distinguished looking men, thoughtful, experienced and so beautiful. Your father's hymn, 'All the Days,' was admirably sung, and the refrain was given with great tenderness. Indeed, the occasion so mournful must be a sweet memory, and was a genuine tribute to one of the saintliest and most eminent of the men of the time. His blessedness is complete. I talked with Dr. Schaff for half an hour a week since. His admiration and regard for your father were sincere and enthusiastic. He deeply regretted his absence in the West at the time of the funeral."

The Rev. Charles S. Robinson, D. D., of New York City, wrote:

"I am very grateful to the family and friends who send me an invitation to be present at the funeral services of Dr. Abraham Coles. I have always had the highest regard for him, and I shall distinctly mourn his unexpected death. I cannot be present at the services on Friday; this I say with real regret. I wish my condolence to be given, and my most respectful regards to be proffered to those who are bereaved."

Gen. Theodore Runyon, ex-Chancellor of New Jersey, writes:

"We were very much pained to learn of the death of your honored and distinguished father, and my wife and I beg to tender to you the assurance of our sincere sympathy and condolence in your great affliction."

The Rev. Henry Clay Trumbull, D. D., of Philadelphia, editor of the "Sunday School Times," though well-nigh crushed with the weight of his own burden of grief and trial, wrote:

"I loved and honored your dear father, and his saintly memory is precious to me, as to many others. May God's blessing be with you 'All the Days.'"

Hiram H. Tichenor, M. D., of Newark, N. J., writes:

"It was my melancholy duty to attend the special meeting of the Essex County Medical Society, held in reference to the death of your lamented father. Let me say that, during my nearly forty years' connection with the Society, I never saw an exhibition of deeper sorrow than on that occasion."

The "New York Observer," in a leading article, says:

"We record with a deep sense of personal loss the death of Dr. Abraham Coles. * * * * His hymn, 'All the Days,' will carry a message of comfort to many a weary heart in years to come."

Rev. T. E. Vassar, D. D., a former pastor of the South Baptist Church, Newark, N. J., of which Dr. Coles was one of the original founders, writes from Kansas City, Missouri, as follows:

"This week's (New York) 'Examiner' which has just reached me, tells me of your great loss. I lay aside all work to assure you of my sincere sympathy in this time of sorrow, and yet to rejoice with you over a father who has so grandly done his work and passed to be forever with his Lord. I know how heavily shadowed your beautiful home must be these bright May days, and I know how for months yet your honored parent will be missed and mourned; but if the present is clouded, the past and the future are more radiant than sun or skies. Around years that are gone hang all sweet and blessed memories, and over the years that lie ahead hangs the glory of a heavenly home. God give you to look this morning in both directions and so to smile amid your tears.

"Very pleasantly I remember the hour enjoyed with your father last August, and distinctly I recall his parting words. He intimated that we might not meet again on earth, but spoke of 'something better further on.' In part, his words have proved true. Let us trust they will prove altogether prophetic. May the Comforter who came to Bethany with His words of life and immortality shed abroad in your hearts His deep, abiding peace."

The Rev. A. H. Lewis, D. D., pastor of the Seventh Day Baptist Church, Plainfield, N. J., and editor of "The Outlook," a Sabbath quarterly, says:

"Accept my wife's and my own sympathy, while we unite in the peace we know must fill your hearts, even though shadowed. To bear the name, and enshrine the memory, of such a father, is a blessing for which others might well long. May the peace of Him who hath welcomed your father into rest abide in your hearts."

The Rev. Aaron H. Burlingham, D. D., Secretary of the American Baptist Missionary Union, wrote:

"I deeply care for you in your great bereavement. How sadly the excursion for pleasure ended in sorrow. To a ripe age, your distinguished and honored father remained with you, but the blow came too soon, by far. May you find support in the only source of comfort—your father's God. Mrs. Burlingham joins me in sympathy with you in this hour of crushing grief."

J. K. Hoyt, formerly associate editor of the "Newark Daily Advertiser," and more recently compiler of the "Cyclopædia of Practical Quotations," published by Funk & Wagnalls, New York, says:

"The first notice of your father's death came to me in Florida. Your father was one of my best friends, and I am happy to say that, I have none but the pleasantest memories of him. He was courteous and kind when I was entirely friendless in Newark, and I shall never forget the pleasant and improving hours at his own home."

The Rev. J. M. Stevenson, D. D., Secretary of the American Tract Society, writes:

"Our family was shocked to see in the daily papers the statement that your good father had suddenly ceased to live here, while on a Western tour. Terrible as the blow must be to you, I am very sure that your confidence, and that of all who knew him, assures you that he now lives a higher and more glorious life; and this is a comfort above all other sources of comfort. While we sympathize most deeply with you in your irreparable loss, accept the strongest expression of our suffering with you."

The Hon. Vice Chancellor Abraham V. Van Fleet gives expression to his heartfelt grief in these words of love and sympathy:

"I am saddened by the news of the death of your father. The death of such a man is a great loss. It would be better for the race if such men could live forever. They make the whole world better.

They soften and refine everything they come in contact with; the influence of their lives is like a benediction. I do not believe that any one ever had a better father."

The Rev. Edgar M. Levy, D. D., of Philadelphia, Penn., says:

"From a notice in the 'National Baptist' I learn, with the deepest sorrow, of the death of your honored father. I can scarcely believe it to be true, yet I fear it is so. Your father was the purest, truest, noblest man I ever knew. His mind was as cultured as his heart was filled with every generous and noble affection. The strength of manhood in him was united to the tenderness and gentleness of woman. I am aware that I am telling nothing which you do not already know, but it affords me some consolation to bear this testimony to my friend and brother, and the friend of her who cannot now join in the expressions of grateful appreciation which, during her life, frequently fell from her lips."

The Rev. D. J. Yerkes, D. D., of Plainfield, N. J., writes:

"It could not have been otherwise than that you should have felt satisfaction in your father's celebrity, earned in his profession and in the walks of literature; but his nobility of character, his manliness, his sweetness of spirit, now that he is gone, makes a precious, immortal memory. He was strong, yet gentle; decided in opinion, yet tolerant; great, but humble; honored of men, while he honored most of all his divine Lord. 'Though dead, he yet speaketh.' The life now ended has left echoes grander than noblest speech, and sweeter than sweetest music."

Prof. Robert T. S. Lowell, D. D., of Schenectady, N. Y., the author and poet, brother of James Russell Lowell, was confined to his room by what proved to be his last sickness, when the news of the death of Dr. Coles reached him; yet he wrote, with effort:

"We are with you in your sorrow, and in your consolation."

Subsequently his faithful daughter, M. A. Lowell, being in constant attendance upon her father, wrote to the daughter of Dr. Coles:

"My father desires me to send to you, and your brother, his last farewell. He feels that he is failing, and cannot stay much longer. I am thankful to think that he is not suffering pain, only excessive weakness."

Hon. David Ayres Depue, LL. D., Justice of the Supreme Court of New Jersey, wrote:

"It has been my good fortune to be reckoned among your father's friends; and, if I could take time from the official duties now pressing me, I would express in an appropriate manner my love and veneration for him, and my admiration for his writings. Fortunately for Dr. Coles' memory, it needs no tribute from any one of his friends."

Clara H. Stranahan, of Brooklyn, N. Y., author of "A History of French Painting, From Its Earliest to Its Latest Practice," etc., writes:

"How glad I personally am now that I had so recently the pleasure and satisfaction of that day's intercourse with your much esteemed father at his home. It stands out as a bright spot in the crowding, passing life. From his 'All the Days' and 'Sweet By and By,' his friends may be comforted and led to renewed struggles for the purity that will assure us that

"'In the Sweet By and By,
We shall meet on that beautiful shore.'

"My husband (Hon. J. S. T. Stranahan) joins me in expressions of deep and sympathetic regard."

Henry C. Bowen's daughter, the light and life of her father's household, yet "acquainted with grief," thus writes to the daughter of Dr. Coles:

"ROSELAND, WOODSTOCK, Conn.

"Upon my return from Europe, not two weeks ago. I learned of the sorrow that has come so recently to you, and I want to reach out my hand with a word of sympathy; for I know, so well, the full meaning of the separation from a dear one, and the long silence that follows. I remember so pleasantly the evening your father spent with us in Brooklyn, when our own hearts were then so happy. What we have suffered since those only know who have tried to endure such a loss; but it is a great deal to have the memory of such companionships. That you must feel, when you look back upon your father's life with you. Such lives are a continual blessing. I often hear of you, though we seldom meet."

Margaret E. Sangster, in alluding to a visit at Deerhurst, speaks as follows:

"Harper & Brothers' Editorial Rooms,
"Franklin Square, New York.

"My recollection of Dr. Abraham Coles is peculiarly delightful. I can see him in his library surrounded by the books which were his tools and companions; and I can even hear him reading musical and solemn lines from his 'Light of the World,' on which he was at work. He has passed from the Delectable Mountains to the City of the King."

The Rev. Edwin W. Rice, D. D., editor of the "Sunday School World," writes from Philadelphia, Pa.:

"There was a depth of Christian experience shown in his correspondence, by your father, which could not fail to impress every mind. There is nothing so strongly manifesting the true Christian, as the spirit of his criticism, and, in this, Dr. Coles was superior to most men that I have known. All that my friends, Drs. Boardman and McArthur, say of him, I found to be true in the best sense."

The Rev. F. M. McAllister, rector of Trinity Church, Elizabeth, N. J., writes:

"I am pleased to read in the public journals the testimonials of appreciation, especially that of the poet Whittier; it was a splendid recognition of your father's literary merit. The exquisite simplicity of your father's Christian trust was so free from the skeptical Pilate question, 'What is truth?' which is abroad to-day, and has in it no confidence, and no reverence, and no respect, but is an impudent cavil against the truth."

The Rev. Alexander McLaren, D. D., writes from Fallowfield, Manchester, England:

"I truly sympathize with you in your sorrow. My own household has long been like yours—one daughter and one son left to comfort a lonely father—and so I can the better understand and feel with you. In my own griefs I have learned, I hope, one lesson—that the only real consolation lies in submission. When we can say, 'Thy will be done,' some peace, which prophesies fuller comfort in due time, begins to dawn upon us. I pray that you and your brother may be able to accept the sorrow, for accepted sorrow is blessed, and is on the way to become, if not joy, at least tranquility."

The Rev. J. W. Sarles, D. D., writes from Stelton, N. J.:

"I am sure a priceless legacy is left you in his memory. How sweetly peaceful was the end! 'Mark the perfect man, and behold the upright; for the end of that man is peace.' 'The memory of the just is blessed.'"

The Rev. George E. Horr, D. D., of Summit, N. J., writes :

"Your father's eminence in learning and art and talent, and the breadth of his knowledge, made it a comfort to have his loving regard. Yours is no common loss. So few, so very few, have stood in such exalted relations to a kingly one in letters, to such exquisite taste, to such tender heartedness, to such rare idealism, and to such wealth of love and beauty. But to think of all these glorified, and that the heart that touched your lives in exalted joy and comfort, waits to add its heavenliness to your communings; and, by and by, to a blissful reunion ! Now tears may dim, yet I am sure the blessings of the past, and those yet to come, with the sainted father, will give a sacred peace and joy."

The Rev. Samuel R. House, M. D., D. D., for many years, with his wife, a missionary of the Presbyterian Board of Foreign Missions, at Bangkok, Siam, writes from Waterford, N. Y.:

"From a newspaper obituary notice I learned of your sad and sudden bereavement. My heart, and my dear wife's, go out towards you in sorrow and sincerest sympathy. I know how much you loved and revered him, and how justly proud you were of the nobility of his character, his gifts, and his graces; and of what he had done and written to instruct and bless the world. * * * * I, too, loved your dear father and felt honored by his kind regard for me and mine. I shall ever esteem it a privilege to have known one I honored so much for his learning, his poetic talent, the consecration of his gifts to his Redeemer; and the pleasure, instruction and helps, I have derived from his writings. Sincerely I shall mourn his loss. * * * * Many may die as sudden, few as safe. He 'knew' in whom he had 'believed.' His Incarnate Lord, into the sweet wonders of whose love he had looked so long, and so studiously, was to him a living presence, and He was with him when he died—the blessed, all glorious Friend, who never forsakes. Yes, if any man, surely, your good father could say, in the words he puts into aged Simeon's mouth:

" 'Master! it is enough. I die in peace,
Thou hast fulfilled Thy promise. Now release
Thy servant when Thou pleasest. For mine eyes,
Have seen the Saviour, and it doth suffice:' *

"And who could more exult than he, when so suddenly faith was exchanged for sight."

William Rankin, a prominent merchant of Newark, N. J., and one active in good works, writes:

" Permit me to add an expression of my high appreciation of your partiality in selecting me as one of the pall-bearers at the funeral of your revered father. * * * * There always seemed a peculiar sympathy between your dear father and myself, when we met, which made our intercourse elevating and Christian. His qualities of heart no less than mind shone conspicuous in his daily life, and I can appreciate to some extent your great loss, and sympathize in that affliction."

* The "Evangel," pp. 73-74.

Rev. Robert P. Kerr, D. D., writes from Richmond, Virginia:

"I deeply sympathize with you in the removal of your father, but your loss is his eternal glory and gain. I knew him, and like every one else, loved him."

Aaron M. Powell, of the Society of Friends, editor of "The Philanthropist," etc., sent the following:

"I sympathize with you deeply in the great void which you must realize in your own life in the loss of such a companionship as that of your father. I congratulate you, also, upon the rich legacy you inherit in so precious a memory. A cultured representative of the old school of Christian gentlemen, his personal presence seemed to me a benediction."

Richard J. Dunglison, M. D., Treasurer of the American Medical Association, writes from Philadelphia, Pa.:

"I heard of your loss with sincere regret. No one admired your father's personal character more than myself, and his published works have often given pleasure to myself and family; for we have frequently read, and re-read, the charming effusions of his true Christian spirit."

The Rev. John Hall, D. D., LL. D., of New York City, says in his letter of sympathy:

"* * * * What a joy it is to think of that home, and the meeting there! Your father's God you will trust and love as yours."

The Rev. Abraham Coles Osborn, D. D., a successful minister of Christ, writes the following, from his field of labor at Albion, N. Y.:

"In a full age, but out of the fullness of health, and happiness, and great usefulness, the Master hath said, 'Come up higher.' With great sincerity, with a high and holy purpose, with transparent honesty, with unceasing and unvarying fidelity, and with great ability, he served his generation. The world is better that he lived in it. If I may say a personal word, my own life has received some of its best impulses, and its highest aspirations, from him whose name I bear. Blessed, thrice blessed, be his memory."

Bishop John H. Vincent, D. D., LL. D., Chancellor of the Chautauqua University, being unable to write himself, by reason of severe illness, dictated a letter, from which we quote two sentences:

"Dr. Coles was a magnificent man, physically, intellectually and spiritually; he was one among ten thousand. * * * * Who can doubt the great doctrines of immortality in the presence of such a life as that of Dr. Abraham Coles."

Rev. Dr. W. C. Stitt, Secretary of the Seaman's Friend Society, wrote:

"76 Wall street, NEW YORK.

"'Servant of God, well done!' is the sweet song of angels over your father's grave. It is the triumphant strain in his children's hearts that subdues their sorrow. Permit me to add my 'Servant of God, well done!' to yours."

Mary Mapes Dodge, editor of "St. Nicholas," etc., concludes her letter of affectionate sympathy in the following words:

"The thought of your dear father's noble character, his long life of usefulness and honor, his pure and exalted nature, and his steadfast faith—this will comfort you. * * * Your father's memory always will be dear and sacred to our family."

Edmund C. Stedman writes:

"I have learned the tidings of your dear, saintly, noble father's death. We knew that it must be ere long, yet I am distressed. I mourn with you that we shall see his beautiful face, his stately figure, no more in this life. * * * * To-night I have been reading one of the most fervent and exquisite letters ever penned—that which he sent me a few days after my mother's death."

Prof. William Garden Blaikie, of New College (Free Church), Edinburgh, in his letter, says:

"9 Palmerston Road, Grange, EDINBURGH.

"You are blessed to have had such a father, and to have such memories of a father."

The Rev. Edward Judson, D. D., writes from Memorial Baptist Church, Washington Square, New York City:

"I loved and admired your father very much. I shall never forget a happy evening I spent with him in Orange, N. J. I have read with deepest interest whatever I have been able to secure from his graceful pen. His rendering of the Psalms I prize most highly. * * * * Sympathizing with you in your inexpressible loss, I remain, yours most sincerely."

Edward Bierstadt, of New York City, says:

"When I read of your loss I was overcome with sorrow. My heart was so full, I could not find words to express my feelings. Your father was the finest and highest type of man I had ever met. He seemed to me to be different from all others. I was often amazed at his vast amount of diversified knowledge. Some men parade their learning—he never did; but you could not ask him a question on any subject, but what you found him to be perfectly familiar therewith. He was a reliable, sterling, good man."

Rev. Josiah Strong, D. D., General Secretary of the Evangelical Alliance for the United States, who, in the words of its President, William E. Dodge, "has the confidence and respect of all the churches," writes from Greenwich, Connecticut:

"Your father's 'Ever, my Lord, with Thee,' 'All the Days,' and other hymns, will now have new meaning to you. I can offer you the sympathy of one who has had the same experience."

The Rev. Henry M. Sanders, D. D., of New York City:

"I had great admiration for your father. His was a sweet and seraphic spirit, unearthly and pure. Death to such a one is only transition."

The Rev. D. R. Frazer, D. D., pastor of the First Presbyterian Church, Newark, N. J., writes:

"Your father had a very large place in my heart. My wife and I often speak of the delightful day spent at your home, and although we realize the desolation which has come to it, yet you can find joy in the fact that your good father rests in the great Father's home on high."

Rev. H. W. Ballantine, D. D., of Bloomfield, N. J.:

"I remember very pleasantly the day, four years ago last spring, and the bright shining of your father's face, as he moved about among his guests, showing us the various treasures of his library. Your bereavement in the loss of such a father is indeed great, but the fact which makes it so contains also its own great consolation. Mrs. Ballantine joins me in sympathy and remembrance."

In the cause of Hungary and Poland, Dr. Coles always took a deep interest. For Kossuth and his talented sister, Madame Ruttkay, the latter a near neighbor and a frequent guest at Deerhurst, Dr. Coles cherished great admiration and respect, as well as friendship.

Ernest A. Von Diezelski, a Polish patriot, a refined and cultivated gentleman, professes to have derived much comfort and instruction from the writings of Dr. Coles; and holds, in grateful remembrance, the words of wisdom, it was his privilege to hear, from the Doctor's own lips. He concludes his letter:

"God grant that we may all look upon death as he did, and be partakers of that peace, even here on earth, of which he was a living testimony."

The Rev. Lyman Abbott, D. D., author, editor of the "Christian Union," etc., wrote:

"I regret that my absence from town prevented me from acknowledging before the receipt of your invitation to the funeral services of Dr. Abraham Coles. Duties here in New York made it impossible for me to attend. Yours sincerely."

Rt. Rev. John Williams, D. D., LL. D., Bishop of the Diocese of Connecticut, Chancellor of Trinity College, etc., writes from Middletown, Conn:

"When I learned of the departure of your dear excellent father, had I known where to write, I should have written at once to say how fully I sympathize with you in your bereavement, and how truly I honored and reverenced him. He was indeed 'a good man, and full of the Holy Ghost.' I always read his delightful writings with pleasure and profit. There was an aroma of purity and godly grace about them that was particularly attractive. The world is richer for such a life as his, and poorer for his loss. But God knows best, and I trust that you will have—I am sure you will—those abounding consolations which only the one great Comforter can give. Believe me, very truly yours."

Rt. Rev. Phillips Brooks, D. D., Bishop of the Diocese of Massachusetts, writing from Boston, in a note full of kindness, uses the following words:

"All that concerns your father is of great interest to me, for I have long known his work and valued it. I send to you my sincerest sympathy. At the same time I rejoice with you in your faith and hope. Faithfully and truly."

Rev. B. Griffith, D. D., General Secretary, editor, and acting Treasurer of the American Baptist Publication Society, writes from Philadelphia concerning the death of Dr. Coles:

"I am both glad and sorry. Glad that God gave you so excellent a father, so truly worthy of your love. I know what it is to lose a father in early life, and can, therefore, sympathize with those who are called to a similar loss. Most heartily do I sympathize with you in this bereavement, but you know the source of refuge, and to that source you have learned the way."

Nathan Haskell Dole, the successful translator of Russian and Spanish works, etc., says in his letter, written from Jamaica Plain, Hedgecote, Glen Road:

"When I saw the notice of your father's passing beyond, I was moved to sit down immediately and write, expressing my sympathies. I shall never forget seeing your father in his library. His stately, serene presence, so dignified, so truly poetical, seemed fitly enshrined in the precious treasures of thought which he had so lovingly collected. Alas! that it was only once to have seen him there! Yet when I read how he had vanished from earth, it seemed as though I had lost something great. How much more must that have seemed to you, who lived in the very sunshine of his life. Words are very feeble to express sympathies. Very cordially yours."

The "Boston Transcript" contained the following contribution from the pen of Elizabeth G. Shepard:

"Abraham Coles dead! Alas, that so brilliant a light should be extinguished. How will the world far and wide weep for him. Physician, surgeon, linguist, author, poet and critic, to him all things seemed possible, and he touched nothing that he did not beautify and adorn. His deep learning, his wondrous genius filled us with admiration, and yet, more than all, one loved him for his great and exceeding goodness. The rare quality of humility was all his own. His writings breathe the strong religious fervor that characterized his life.

"I remember 'The Microcosm' in the possession of a friend who is a physician. So highly did he prize it, that it was most jealously guarded, and although he would read to us from its pages, it was always reluctantly yielded to our touch. The book was a favorite, it was rare, and belonged to him. Some time after, it was with pardonable pride I could write that not only did I own the book, but it had been presented to me by the author.

"The home of Doctor Coles, 'Deerhurst,' at Scotch Plains, New Jersey, has always abounded in hospitality; one was sure of a most

cordial welcome from the kindly host, his son, and daughter, who gracefully presided over her father's establishment. Surrounded by broad acres the mansion is substantial, elegant and beautiful, and is replete with articles rich and rare that have been gathered in frequent journeyings through foreign lands. Back from the house a short distance, is the deer park, and the older and more sedate creatures gaze at us with beautiful soft eyes, while the timid fawn dashes off with graceful leap and bound. Farther on is the labyrinth, a fac-simile of the famous one at Hampton Court, and as we wandered through the intricate passages, how demurely did Doctor Coles follow us, giving no hint as we strayed from the right way, until, after many a twist and turn and new departure, we finally reached the goal in the centre. And then how delightful to rest there, and listen to the glowing eloquence of him whom we now mourn!

"The remembrance comes of another day, when after a brisk canter over level roads, we alighted beneath the port-cochère, and mounting the massive stairway, entered the Doctor's study, the door of which was thrown hospitably wide open. The very atmosphere seemed inspiring, for here were stored the richest thoughts and sweetest inspirations the world has known. The room is open to the roof, the oaken rafters coming down in graceful sweeps, with here and there odd little windows, deeper ones reaching to the floor and opening upon slender balconies and vine-clad verandas. On every side are books: in massive cases, filling deep recesses, on shelves substantially built around corners and supported by ornamental columns, and on daintier shelves arranged above one's head. A vast and varied collection, carefully and worthily bound. What a genial welcome awaited us! and it was the most alluring armchair that was wheeled into the most comfortable position for us, while Doctor Coles, seated at his study table, read from the manuscript his criticism upon Stedman's 'Poets of America.'

"But with these pleasurable recollections comes the sad realization of sorrow and bereavement. No more can we enjoy the living presence, never again bask in the sunshine of his glorious intellect. To those near and dear to him the loss is irreparable; the very sunlight must to them seem blasted.

"We mourn; but there will come the consolation that we are in possession of his inspirations, of the fruits of his untiring industry, and that for him there is fulfillment."

ADDITIONAL SELECTIONS

FROM THE

WORKS OF ABRAHAM COLES.

A NEW YEAR'S GREETING.

A HAPPY New Year to you all:
    In answer to my humble call,
On your dear heads may blessings fall
    From Heavenly Friend,
Without a moment's interval,
    To the Year's end.

O, there is breath, that's more than breath,
A prayer that saith more than it saith,
The prayer of prayer, the prayer of faith,
    That prayer I pray,
(Which the heart only uttereth)
    To God to-day!

That love is poor the heart can speak,
The language of the lips is weak,
No organ hath true love, we seek
    In vain t' impart
(Though ours the master tongue of Greek)
    Th' unuttered heart.

As one great instrumental whole,
Responsive to divine control,
The spheres make music as they roll;
    O, like to this,
Those sweet vibrations of the soul
    Where true love is!

A NEW YEAR'S GREETING.

When summer melts the selfish frost,
How like a prince—disdaining cost,
Counting for love the world well lost—
    The yearning breast
Would the full universe exhaust
    To make one blest!

When spoils of Nature and of Art
Have all been lavished, still, O Heart!
Esteeming this the smallest part,
    Thy fond desire
Would into unseen regions dart
    For something higher.

Even so, my wishes upward rise,
On wings of prayer above the skies,
To bring that good, God's grace supplies
    To sinful men,
From that dear bosom, where it lies,
    To you, Amen!

HARMONY.

How good, how pleasant, nought can it excel,
    For brethren all in unity to dwell;
T' agree to differ; since while man is man,
There must be difference, do what we can.
How petty oft the causes that divide—
Some little nothing fondly magnified,
Less than a letter, roughness of the breath,
A mere unasperated Shibboleth:
Brothers in all agreeing, all the same,
Save in the pronunciation of a name.
Vain are our wranglings, easy 't were to prove,
He fails in every thing who fails in Love.
Let men reserve anathemas for sin,
Lies and hypocrisies concealed within;
And excommunicate from Church and State
That great heresiarch whose name is Hate.

THE REDEEMER.

YE fair and fadeless Stars, that hither turn
    All your converging and sweet wondering eyes
From every part of the surrounding heavens,
Holding compassionate and patient watch,
Pure witnesses of all the births of Time
From man's apostasy until this hour!—
Now join to celebrate with the redeemed,
The Saviour's advent to this far off Earth,
Who came that He might bring the lost one back,
Back from the hungry, fiery jaws of Hell,
To shine once more in your bright neighborhood.
Unchanged amid all changes, lo! ye smile
And send serene and loving glances down,
(For hate ye cannot) owning still the bonds
Of sympathy and sisterhood, despite
Her blurred and altered phase and depth of shame.

  Ye deem it ill becomes you to contemn
What the Creator cares for. Ye are pure,
But not so pure as He, yet His delights

Have from the first been with the sons of men,
Whose utter ruin left unmeasured scope,
For a display of love, transcending all
That highest Seraphim had ever thought.
Yea! Earth from all eternity He willed
Should be the honored theatre whereon
The Godhead should surmount the loftiest scale
Of possibilities of grace.   Ye dim
And twinkling orbs! ye that are sunk most far
In the deep ether, must have heard the fame
Of that stupendous miracle—a Child
Of Virgin born, His name Emmanuel,
In whom the fullness of the Godhead dwelt,
Whose birth to shepherds first announced, what time
They watched their flocks upon Judea's hills
Beneath your smiling and rejoicing beams.
O, stole ye not a glimpse of the sweet Babe,
As in the manger lying, underneath
The Mother's doting and adoring eye,
And stooped yourselves to do him homage?   For
The might, that formed and whirls you on your way,
Was there pent up within that Infant Form;

That puny arm sustained the Universe;
That tongue, which then was mute, had power to change
Th' abiding laws of Nature and of Fate.

   Years rolled away: meanwhile, this Wondrous Child
Had grown to manhood's stature—marred his form,
His visage ploughed with grief. Much had He toiled
And suffered. Him full often had ye seen
Through tedious hours of night, engaged in prayer,
Alone, in mountain solitudes. Sometimes,
An awful majesty broke forth through His
Accustomed meekness. Now His voice was heard
Chiding the storm-tossed sea and raging winds
That gave obsequious heed; and now, the dead
Waking, as from slight slumber, at a word;
And now, forgiving sin, as highest proof,
Maugre that guise of weakness, He was God.

   Remember ye Gethsemane? We said,
Of mortal sorrow He had drunk full cup;
But there ye saw Him prostrate, crying out,
"Father, if possible, let this cup pass!"
His grief, that waxed intenser day by day,

Had reached its acme. Gracious God! a sweat
Of blood, wrung out by pressure of His agony
"Dipped Him all o'er," a dreadful baptism, but
For whose accomplishment He yet had longed.
He stood the Atlas of a sinking world,
By guilt so ponderous grown, that, even He
Who holds Creation up, one moment seemed
To stagger 'neath it and to fail of strength.

Ye saw another scene, at midday too.
A preternatural darkness wrapt the land
For three hours' space, and ye looked down
On Calvary, a hill hard by Jerusalem.
O sight of horror! O atrocious deed!
There hung th' incarnate God, besmeared
With blood and spittal, haggard, most forlorn,
Writhing in helpless agony. Shocked and aghast,
Withdrew ye not your shining in that hour,
The darkest from eternity, and yet
The brightest, hour most signal, big with fate,
The fate of countless millions? Blood there spilt
Quenched everlasting fires! 'Twas proof of love
Amazing Heaven and Earth and even Hell.

Though ye're all lustrous and immaculate,
The brightest were, I trow, ne'er honored thus.
Ye have, perhaps, angelic visitants, but when
Did God descend among you, and become
As one of your own people; not a guest,
But denizen and fellow through long years?
The fruit of so mysterious and matchless grace,
Is not yet fully reaped. Hereafter, ye
Shall see the renovated earth shine forth
Fair as the fairest and as blest as erst.

    CHRISTMAS, 1851.

THE FUTURE LIFE.

ON the strong pinions of the fleeting Years,
    We all are borne unceasingly aloft,
Straight toward the azure of Eternity.
That infinite and all-embracing Cope
Of Mystery, we soon shall penetrate,
And be as gods in knowledge. We who now

THE FUTURE LIFE.

Are ignorance and feebleness, blind moles
That burrow in the ground, are destined yet
To know as we are known. Each gordian knot
And awful problem of our being solved,
Dwelling in light forever. Can it be?
Ay, even so! Bear witness, Earth and Heaven!
If myriads such as we are have not passed,
Upon the Bosom of the Year just flown,
Up thence into the Infinite; though now
No more incarnate; for that flesh and blood
Cannot inherit it, nor yet abide
So awful an amazement, as there smites
The soul, amid the uncovered mysteries
Of that illimitable and dread domain.
Unless of fleshly garment all unclothed,
And clothed with other and adapted garb,
Like that which spirits wear, who could behold,
With unaccustomed eyes, the naked face
Of the immediate Godhead, and yet live!
Not Seraphim or Cherubim dare look,
Familiarly, with bold and open gaze,
Nor but with timid awe and shaded brow,
Upward to that high throne on which He sits,
So blinding is the brightness, piercing, pure.

Should one of earthly mould, with mortal weakness girt,
Intrude in that Dread Presence, how at once
Would he, both by the lightning and the light,
Be all transfixed and panged in every part,
All scorched and blasted and consumed away!
But disembodied spirits at this hour
Are passing thence, made able to endure
The infinite amazement. O my soul!
What shuts thee out this moment from the sight,
Except this crumbling wall of fragile flesh,
Now weakly tottering, on which Time beats
Unceasingly, exposed besides to all
The thousand shocks of mortal accident?
This hindrance broken down, ah! then, thou too
Shalt meet those piercing and perusing eyes,
That judge thee while they search thee; hear that voice,
Which shakes the universe; that spake
The all-creating fiat, breaking first
The everlasting silence; that pronounced,
With stern and dreadful emphasis of wrath,
Then first provoked, the Malison and Doom,
That down to just damnation sank for aye
The apostate sons of heaven, of which the sound
Through all the infernal caverns echoes still.

THE FUTURE LIFE.

What tremblings and what swoonings of dismay,
Await us, in that solemn hour, that opes
The portals of Eternity, and o'er
Its mystic threshold bears and shuts us in—
The hour of birth into another life!
Sooner or later it must come to all.
But who so dastard or so groveling,
As e'er to wish 'twere less inevitable,
As not to hail it though so full of dread?
Immortal Thought—uncrowded and unchecked
By the insulting and encroaching banks
Of scooped material channels, that sometime
Did shore and shallow it—shall then burst forth,
O'erflowing and redundant as a sea;
And in its liquid, clear, unfathomed depths
Shall be reflection and solution seen
Of endless Mysteries of the Universe;
All former truth and knowledge, though as great
As Newton boasted, being swallowed up
And lost, as rain-drops in the ocean. Stars
And Suns innumerable—not as here
By distance dimmed and dwindled, but full-orbed
And unimaginably bright—above its vast
Immeasurable horizon, lo! shall rise

And set no more forever. From the face
Of all things, shall be lifted and rolled off
The wide concealing darkness, laying bare
The mighty hand of casual Deity,
Beneath the deep foundations of the world
Swift touching all the springs of harmony.
In vain search wearied, groping evermore
In guessing ignorance, or with blind plunge
Leaping despairingly we know not where,
How blessed, how divine, to rest tired feet
On the Eternal Rock of Certainty!

O, most exalted fate of man! the Soul,
That with invincible instinct yearned to know,
Thus privileged, within the Azure Veil,
Into the Unprofaned and Holy Place
And secret Sanctuary of the Sky
To look—yea! unforbidden pass the high
Once inaccessible threshold, to the Shrined,
Adorable Wonder and the All in All;
To climb the Heaven of Heaven, the Height of Heights,
And from supremest altitudes, with keen
And multipresent faculty behold
Creation all in prospect, seen at once;

THE FUTURE LIFE.

Or, with accompanying Archangel, soar
On sociable swift wing, so swift scarce sight
Can follow or thought overtake, far thence
To the dim frontiers and extremest bounds
Of starred immensity, along the bright
And blazing pathway of unnumbered worlds,
Rolling forever in their mighty orbs—
Waving glad pinions to th' eternal chime
Of sphere-born harmonies; now lost
In the effulgence of some central Sun,
Dispenser of wide day to planets round,
As briefly stooping holy feet to bathe
In luminous fountains full as at the first,
By the fierce heat and radiance unconsumed;—
Emerging sparkling thence, limbs dripping light,
And trailing splendors through the Ethereal Deep,
With unstayed wing, till on the shore arrived
Of Chaos, void and without form and dark,
They stand spectators of creative acts,
Hear sounding through th' abyss once more
Th' omnific word: "Let Be!" to unborn worlds.

The immaterial Spirit, fed with strength
Unfailing, knows no weariness, and needs

Nor sleep nor rest, but buoyant, fresh,
Throughout the lapse of unimaginable years,
Without one void oblivious moment, works.
And as one day is as a thousand years
To Him who fills Eternity, yet finds
In every moment room enough to be,
Ev'n so to man—in that immortal realm,
With his accelerated powers of thought,
(Since Time is being, measured by the whirl
Of consciousness as well as circling spheres,
By varying states of mind made swift or slow)—
In the expanded limits of an hour,
May ages of existence seem to roll,
As marvelously prefigured oft in dreams.

   In that so multiplied Eternity,
Among such scenes, and fellowships, and acts
Of godlike power and glory, and events
Without a name or parallel on earth,
O what a History! O what a Life!
Must thence arise to our immortal selves—
Amid all changes consciously the same,
Our cradled ignorance remembered still

To swell the wonder of the distance passed,
And make us humbler, as we higher rise,
Godward, in grand interminable ascent
Of knowledge, goodness, purity, and love.

NEW YEAR, 1842.

HYMNS FOR WHITSUNDAY.*

NEW TRANSLATIONS.

THE following hymns, addressed to the Holy Spirit, the Paraclete, the incomparable gifts, poured out in baptismal fulness on the day of Pentecost in fulfillment of the promise of the Father, are appropriate to the present season. A cry for help to the Supreme Helper, they have served to voice the need of successive generations uninterruptedly for a thousand years. The authorship of the first is attributed to Charlemagne.

*For other versions, see "Old Gems in New Settings," and "The Light of the World."

Its worth and dignity are attested by its use on all occasions of unusual solemnity, as the coronation of kings, the ordination of priests, the consecration of bishops, the celebration of synods and the creation of popes. It has been translated by Dryden and others. The second hymn is ascribed to Robert II, King of France. Archbishop Trench calls it "the loveliest of all the hymns in the whole circle of Latin sacred poetry."

VENI CREATOR SPIRITUS.

TRANSLATION.

Creator Spirit, condescend
To be our Guest, come, Heavenly Friend!
The breasts Thou hast created fill
With gracious might to do Thy will.

Great Gift of God, the Paraclete,
Well-spring of Life, baptismal Heat,
Love shed abroad to purify,
Omniscient unction from on high!

Thy seven-fold* gifts to us dispense,
Finger of God's omnipotence!

---

* The seven gifts of the Holy Spirit are: 1. Wisdom; 2. Understanding; 3. Counsel; 4. Fortitude; 5. Knowledge; 6. Piety; 7. Fear of God.

Thou who didst once enrich the lungs
With Pentecostal gift of tongues,

Enlighten Thou our darkened powers,
Pour love into these hearts of ours.
Strengthen our body, weak and frail,
With virtue that shall never fail.

Drive Thou the enemy afar,
And give us peace and end the war.
Be Thou our Leader, go before,
So following Thee we'll stray no more.

On us intelligence bestow,
The Father and the Son to know,
Spirit of Both, be still our creed,
Thou dost from Both alike proceed.

Veni Sancte Spiritus.

TRANSLATION.

Holy Spirit, Source of Day,
Come Thou and from heaven a ray
  Of Thy splendor downward dart,

Come, Thou Father of the poor,
Giver of gifts and blessings sure,
  Come, Thou Light of every heart.

Comforter of mortal dole!
Sweet Thy visits to the soul,
  Sweet refreshment, sweet relief:
Thou in labor givest rest,
Coolness to the heated breast,
  Solace in all times of grief.

O most blessed Light divine!
In the heart's recesses shine,
  And with grace Thy faithful fill!
To Thy favoring aid is due
All in man that's good and true,
  Every thing that is not ill.

What is sordid purify,
Duly moisten what is dry,
  Heal Thou what is hurt and sore!
What is stubborn make Thou meek,
Foster what is faint and weak,
  What is wandering restore!

To Thy faithful gracious be,
Trusting evermore in Thee,
  Give to them the sacred seven!
Give them virtue's glorious prize,
Give safe exit to the skies,
  Give the eternal joy of heaven!

JUNE 4th, 1881.

THE SOWER.

A HUSBANDMAN went forth to sow:
  And, as with measured step, he swung
An arm of vigor to and fro,
  The seed he flung.

Some by the wayside fell, thence soon
  By birds devoured, not taking root:
On rocky places some, hot noon
  Withered the shoot:

Some among choking thorns: but seed
  That into good ground fell, behold!

Sprung up and brought forth fruit with speed
    An hundred fold.

O Saviour! lest devouring bird,
  Or shallow soil, or choking thorn,
Frustrate the mercy of Thy word,
    Make sure the corn!

FOREFATHERS' DAY.*

THAT famous Egg of Plymouth Rock,
  Laid by a fowl of noble stock,
Was hatched about that time o'clock,
    They stepped ashore—
The pastor and his little flock
    The Mayflower bore.

A sample egg, a pattern food,
  Un Œuf, that as a feast is good,

---

* Read in response to the sentiment, "All Honor to the Egg that hatched the American Eagle," December 21, 1868, before the New England Society of Newark, N. J., on the occasion of the Anniversary of the Landing of the Pilgrim Fathers on Plymouth Rock, December 10, 1620, O. S.

A grand *egg*-sample *set:* fain would
    Men imitate;
Get eagles' eggs, too, if they could,
    And incubate.

For never yet was there a thing,
So swift, so sure, so bold of wing,
As that proud Bird whose praise I sing—
    Imperial sweep
Of wide-spread pinions, hovering
    O'er land and deep.

"Mewing her mighty youth," and wise,
And kindling her undazzled eyes
At the full midday beam, she flies
    From her high nest,
O'er half the globe, mid changing skies,
    From East to West.

The lagging wind she far outstrips,
Sailing the air as sail the ships,
O'er prairies broad and mountain tips,
    Nor stays her flight,
Till she in either Ocean dips
    Her wing of might.

Where is the acorn, there's the tree:
What is, gives birth to what's to be:
The germ enfolds maturity,
    Life upward leaps:
In that small speck, I dimly see,
    A Nation sleeps—

A bark, lo! sailing o'er the foam,
In which our grave Forefathers come,
To find in western wilds a home—
    Good seed they bear:
They sow the fat and virgin loam
    In faith and prayer.

A handful of the heavenly grain,
Scattered on all the winds with pain,
Is nourished by the dew and rain:
    On every side
It springs, and then is sown again
    And multiplied.

O fruitful is a holy thought!
The planted truth comes not to naught
But with all blessedness is fraught,
    Makes glad the sod:

Behold, what wonders it has wrought,
    The Truth of God!

The wilderness is full of bloom,
And flowers send up a sweet perfume,
And everywhere is seen, in room
    Of rock and brier,
Tilled corn-fields, rich by labor's doom,
    And curse of fire.

Thicket and brake no more conceal
The ancient foes of human weal,
The adder, striking at the heel
    With poisoned fang:
Where Industry's unresting wheel,
    There war-whoop rang.

And Freedom's sun shines clear and bright,
Through clouds that erst obscured its light;
While, from red fields of stormy fight,
    Triumphant comes,
With banners streaming, lo! the Right
    With beat of drums.

Alas! from Sin what sufferings flow!
We reap the misery we sow;

Make Nature's friendly powers our foe;
    By false lights steer:
The fatal cause of all our woe
    Is here, is here.

So sunk in folly is the race,
So sceptical, profane and base,
Man flings the lie in nature's face,
    Calls evil, good:
Loves death: on poison feeds, in place
    Of wholesome food.

From the world's heart profoundly springs,
How vice is venomous and stings,
And none escapes the pain it brings:
    No human tact
Can change the eternal truth of things,
    Make falsehood, fact.

Yet, everywhere, we victims meet,
Of so preposterous a conceit,
That they th' Omniscient God can cheat,
    And trick His laws:—
Though Hell gapes hungry at their feet,
    They will not pause.

The sons of license deem we prate,
Unfolding horrors that await
The souls of them who Wisdom hate,
    But, past a doubt,
The grim, inexorable Fate
    Will find them out.

Death is the price—read Nature's pages—
And she, with all her wealth, engages
To pay to Sin no other wages.
    The Universe
Pledges it naught through all the ages
    Except its curse.

Great are Thy judgments, and unsaid!
Lord! at the nodding of Thy head,
The pillared sky doth shake with dread!
    When cried th' opprest
Vainly to man, Thou cam'st instead
    In vengeance drest.

"Right aiming thunderbolts," forth went,
Flying, as from a bow well-bent,
Out of the clouds, with angry rent
    Cleaving the dark,

Flaming across a Continent,
  Straight to the mark—

And crashing smote, and did not spare,
Laying the earth's foundations bare,
Toppling the shameless Falsehood there,
  And Slavery fell—
A fire, consuming everywhere,
  Burned down to hell.

And folly blamed the Puritan,
That God is God, and man is man;
That thistles grow not figs, nor can:
  The atheist
Mumbled in vain his bitter ban,
  And shook his fist.

Condemned, as we have been, to hear
The echo of a foolish sneer,
From men and boys, for many a year,
  We would beseech,
That they relieve th' afflicted ear
  From further speech.

Your Sires had failings not a few;
"New England Tragedies" were true;
But give the blessed Sun his due,
    Though he have spots!
How bright his beams beneath the blue,
    Despite his blots!

The trafficker in moral wares,
Counts rubbish, and so cheaply spares
The things for which a good man cares—
    'Tis liberal, wise:
Patches the rents in earth's affairs
    By compromise:

Profanely storms the heavenly towers
But jealous, strict, supernal Powers
Forbid we give what is not ours;
    The Godhead toss—
As one on beggars pennies showers—
    Not feeling loss.

Slayer of dragons in his day,
St. George of England did not slay
Old Prejudice, that lives alway:

  Truth oft has tried
To pierce, in many a fierce affray,
   His scaly side.

But Love can do what Truth cannot;
Heaped on the head her coals are hot;
Forget ye what can be forgot!
   Weigh not each feather!
Willing your private griefs to blot,
   Shake hands together!

Ring, Christmas bells, ring merrily!
Ring, *Christus natus hodie!*
The Christ that is and is to be!
   Ring, brotherhood!
Ring, peace! ring, love! ring, jubilee!
   Ring, reign of good!

THE SCOTCH PLAINS.*

FROM Scotland the first settlers came—
    And thence our village has its name—
Exiles for conscience—some, no shame,
    From Scottish jails,
Here wafted, men of honest fame,
    By stormy gales.

They came here with unfettered hands:
To conquer and to bind the lands:
Earth felt how strong the twisted bands
    Of honest toil;
And meekly bent to their commands,
    Lords of the soil.

They dreamed not—none were so brain-sick—
Grain could be grown by any trick—
A conjurer's wand is but a stick,
    A grand deceit—

* Written and read by Dr. Abraham Coles, at the Centennial Anniversary of the completion of the stone Parsonage of the Baptist Church at the Scotch Plains, New Jersey, July 31st, 1886.

Seed must by labor be made quick,
    Ere waves the wheat.

Blame not the churlishness of fields,
If poor returns your labor yields;
The sovereign hand the planet wields
    Is God's, not ours;
In secret cells, the weed conceals
    Great healing powers.

Unkempt, uncultured, wild and rude,
Nature was meant to be subdued,
Through arts industriously pursued,
    By men born poor—
Trained from the first by fortitude,
    Strong to endure.

Know, sons of labor! stalwart, strong,
Ye to a royal line belong!
Your sweaty brows are crowned in song:
    The singing sod
And cities built declare, not wrong,
    You kings to God.

You stretch a sceptre to the skies,
And, lo, what miracles surprise!
Stars for you fight, suns set and rise—
    Obedient powers
Make barren wastes a Paradise
    Of fruits and flowers.

Labor is duty none may shirk:
Great things and noble therein lurk.
"My Father worketh and I work,"
    Our Master said.
It surely ought not you to irk
    To earn your bread.

You are the capitalists—you hold
The talisman that turns to gold,
Who keep the laws ordained of old—
    Deem them no clog—
Who buy and sell, but keep unsold
    The Decalogue.

Their eyes have long been closed in sleep,
Who saw the trembling of the Deep,
Heard howling tempests o'er them sweep,

Till, safe ashore,
Their hearts began to bound and leap,
    With joy once more.

Upon these Plains, where roamed the deer,
Their care was first the ground to clear;
Rude dwellings in these wilds to rear,
    They worked long hours;
But sweet their smile, their joy sincere,
    No doubt, as ours.

God-fearing men and women they,
Who had been taught at home to pray,
And holy keep the Sabbath-day.
    They save, hoard, plod,
Till, having gained the means to pay,
    They build to God.

They humbly built, for they were few;
But "they built better than they knew;"
Their work shall last the ages through:
    Maternal corn,
From handful sown, amazed we view
    Great harvests born.

Things done for Christ the centuries span,
Ye Churches Metropolitan,*
Know ye your being here began?
    How dear the breast
On which thine infancy, O man!
    Was rocked to rest!

When you sat on your mother's knee,
She, possibly, did not foresee
Your urban greatness: but then ye
    Need feel no shame;
Her patent of nobility
    From Virtue came.

Their Meeting-House now made complete,
Thither they weekly turned their feet,
Expecting there their Lord to meet—
    Two sermons hear—
For, oh! the Word of God is sweet
    To hungry ear.

They loved their Minister, aware
He daily in his arms of prayer
Up to the throne of God them bare.

---

* The First Baptist Church of New York City was an offshoot of the Scotch Plains Church.

THE SCOTCH PLAINS.

  The war was past,*
So, for his use they reared with care
  A Manse to last.

They built of stone, the act was brave;
They who had fought the Land to save,
Though by war's desolating wave
  Of much bereft—
Still generous portion freely gave
  Of what was left.

One Hundred Years have passed since then;
While themes for the historic pen
Have been supplied, once and again—
  Three bloody wars,
Enacted in the sight of men
  And blushing stars.

The monster Slavery is slain,
But at what dreadful cost of pain!

*The war for American Independence extended from April 18, 1775, to November 3, 1783. Washington resigned as Commander-in-Chief, December 23, 1783. Federal Constitution was ratified, June 25, 1788. Washington was elected President, January, 1789.

> Would God that other hateful chain
>   Could broken be—
> Intemperance—and men attain
>   True Liberty!
>
> Whom Christ makes free is free indeed:
> This part of Paul, th' Apostle's Creed
> Preach! ye whose business 'tis to plead,
>   And souls to win.
> Tell, how He by five wounds did bleed
>   To free from sin.

THE SCOTCH PLAINS.

RETURN AFTER ABSENCE.

> I TREAD once more my native Plain;
>   I live my childhood o'er again;
> I, who sometimes have mourned with tears,
> The unreturning flight of years,
> Feel the same breezes round me now,
> That fanned in infancy my brow;

And seeing naught that speaks of change,
In wood, or field, or mountain range,
Unconscious of the lapse of days.
The past comes back, and with me stays;
The intervening time forgot,
The absent here, the present not.

How sweetly peaceful and how still!
A Sabbath seems the air to fill;
No sound disturbs the sacred calm,
Save whisper of a plaintive psalm
Made by the leaves, as softly stirred
By the west wind; or song of bird;
Or chirp of insect in the grass;
Or buzz of bees as on they pass
To sip the nectar of the flowers,
Fair birth of vernal suns and showers;
No faculty of soul or sense,
But feels the blessed influence.

Familiar scenes around me start,
Familiar to my eyes and heart;
While every well-known object seems
Tinged with the atmosphere of dreams;

THE SCOTCH PLAINS.

By memory's visionary ray—
More potent than the light of day.
Subtler than that of moon or star,
Which merely show things as they are—
I see o'er all, a glory cast,
A halo borrowed from the past,
Not lifeless forms in tree and stone,
But power and passions not their own.

I once more, as in former time,
The neighboring mountain's summit climb,
And feel, as erst, the matchless charm
Of woodland and of cultured farm;
Of fields of corn and grassy mead,
Where pasturing herds in quiet feed;
Where hand of toil its task achieves
To rear the haycock, bind the sheaves;
And ploughman whistles to the gale;
And milkmaid blithe sings o'er the pail;
And whip-poor-will, and house-dog's bark,
Make glad the coming on of dark.

Where smoke of village upward curls,
There lived old playmates, boys and girls,

And men who long have passed away,
Whose homes remain, but ah! not they.
Hard by yon humble church, are seen
Their rounded graves with rank grass green,
O death! whose desolating tide
Has snatched already from my side
A father, sister, brother, wife—
Long spare me her who gave me life,
My mother, tenant of yon roof,
Loving and good, by every proof.

I wander by the shaded stream,
Where I was wont to sit and dream
Long silent hours, from morn till noon,
Or till the rising of the moon,
In waking visions lost, perchance,
Of poetry and sweet romance;
Or, in devoutest ecstasy—
All conscious of the Deity,
Most present in these solitudes—
Thrilled with the murmur of the woods,
As though it were His voice I heard,
His breath that all the tree-tops stirred.

PRAYER IN AFFLICTION.

If I have traveled o'er the sea,
Been awed by its sublimity;
Seen monuments and cities old;
And mountains soaring in the cold:
Dumb with adoring wonder, stood
Beneath Niagara's thundering flood,
And felt, how awful was the place
Where Godhead met me face to face—
I do not therefore you despise,
Ye're no less lovely in my eyes,
Scenes, first beheld! still, in your face,
I find a glory and a grace.

AUGUST, 1852.

PRAYER IN AFFLICTION.

SINCE dust to Deity may speak,
    I come, O God! with bleeding breast;
Hot tears fast falling on my cheek,
    Dissolving manhood; heaving chest;
And quivering lip that unexpressed
    Leaves words and utters only sighs—
The greatness of my grief attest,
    Grief steeped in bitterest memories.

PRAYER IN AFFLICTION.

I need not tell Thee she is dead,
   Cold in the church-yard, who to me
Was as all earthly joys instead—
   My wife, my lost felicity.
I stretch forth vacant arms to Thee,
   The while my heart makes bitter moan,
That I no more her form shall see,
   That I must tread life's path alone.

Thy brilliant boon of love and bliss,
   In her bestowed, is mine no more;
O help my heart to bow to this.
   To trust, to tremble, and adore!
For she, called mine, was Thine before,
   Nor did my merit title give,
Else wouldst Thou now the lost restore,
   And cause the dead again to live.

II.

O, she was all a wife should be!
   Albeit her thoughts were meekly bent
On household good and piety,

What life so sweetly eloquent,
Or so acceptable to Thee,
  As one in humble duty spent!

If not to dazzle with the play
  Of wit was hers, she knew to bless,
With smiles as cheerful as the day,
  And looks of love and tenderness;
Maintaining thus by happiest art,
  Perpetual sunshine in the heart.

'Twas not the fading charms of face,
  That riveted Love's golden chain;
It was the high celestial grace
  Of goodness, that doth never wane—
Whose are the sweets that never pall,
  Delicious, pure, and crowning all.

III.

Now she is gone! now she is gone!
  Her, thickest night doth ever shroud
From mortal view, and I'm like one
  Whose "welfare passeth as a cloud."

PRAYER IN AFFLICTION.

Lo! I too go with sorrow bowed
    To the dim land of shadows, where
She waiteth, haply, 'mid the crowd
    Of coming souls, my entrance there.

Yet were it better far to think,
    She's now my glistering angel guard,
Still joined by love's unsevered link,
    And near to keep aye watch and ward—
Thy swift winged messenger, O Lord!
    To bear me good, to banish ill,
Along life's pathway, steep and hard,
    My solace, friend, and help-meet still.

O, that my smitten heart may gush
    Melodious praise—like as when o'er
Æolian harp-strings wild winds rush,
    And all abroad sad music pour,
So sweet, Heaven's minstrelsy might hush
    Brief time to listen—for I know
The hand, that doth my comforts crush,
    Builds bliss upon the base of woe.

PRAYER IN AFFLICTION.

If thine own Son was perfect made,
    Through suffering deep as hell's abyss,
And light afflictions here are paid
    With an eternal weight of bliss;
Sure I, unmurmuring, should kiss
    Thy rod of judgment, patient climb
The Mount of Pain, content that this
    Leads gradual to Thy seat sublime.

The time is near, when all shall seem,
    That men pursue with ceaseless thirst,
The vainest nothings of a dream,
    Or phantoms by wild madness nurst:
Then when of life I know the worst,
    And death his stroke shall not defer,
On my rapt soul perchance shall burst,
    The vision bright of Heaven and her.

The murmur of my whispered prayer
    Fails not to reach Thy listening ear—
Though sounds unnumbered fill the air,
    It o'er them all swells loud and clear,

Proceeds it but from heart sincere,
    All crushed and contrite, yielding thence
A pleasing fragrance, far more dear
    Than sweetest smoke of frankincense.

NEWARK, September, 1845.

ON THE DEATH OF PRESIDENT GARFIELD.

LET every weeping Muse draw near,
    For sad and grievous reason,
And lift a soft melodious wail
    To solemnize the season;
Attune to sorrow lyre and voice—
    A mournful duty urges—
And mingle low elegaic moan
    With loud Atlantic dirges.

See, how the land, all stripped to-day
    Of yesterday's adorning,
Sits, like a widow in her weeds,
    Arrayed in deepest mourning!

ON THE DEATH OF GARFIELD.

What means this universal black,
   That clothes all public places,
And darkens all our private homes,
   And glooms all hearts and faces?

The Nation's choice, the Nation's Chief,
   Who was so long in dying,
All stark and stiff and cold in death,
   Is in his coffin lying.
At dead of night were heard the bells
   Of all the church towers tolling,
While Ocean with his thousand waves
   A requiem was rolling.

"He was a man exceeding wise
   Fair spoken and persuading,"
All the divided strands of truth
   With facile fingers braiding.
He in the wrestle of debate
   Knew all the arts of throwing—
The river of mellifluous speech
   In mighty current flowing.

ON THE DEATH OF GARFIELD.

He loved his country, and his life
    He placed upon her altar,
Nor did he e'er in danger's hour,
    In field or forum falter.
But, O, the irony of fate,
    Sad ending of the story,
Quenched was his sun just as it reached
    The zenith of his glory.

God did not mean that human hands
    Should wield the dreadful thunder,
Yet fools and knaves now mimic power
    That rives the rocks asunder.
O hand accursed, forever red!
    Which slew the righteous Abel,
"That fired the shot heard round the world,"
    And clothed the earth in sable.

The pendulum of hope and fear
    Was this and that way swinging,
Through weary weeks, while keenest grief,
    The Nation's heart was wringing.

ON THE DEATH OF GARFIELD.

But when the thread more slender grew
    On which hung in suspension
The wounded life, and day by day
    Was seen a sure declension,

And deadlier grew the poisoned air,
    And summer's heat more galling,
He heard the Ocean from afar,
    With myriad voices calling.
The breezes of a thousand years
    From off the sea were blowing,
And the sick blood and wasted frame
    Were absolute for going.

But flying winds that brought the ships
    Convoyed no gift of healing;
And heaven refused to grant the prayer
    Of millions, jointly kneeling.
To die was better, death was gain
    To him of meek behavior—
Transported to the loving arms
    And bosom of his Saviour.

SEPTEMBER 24, 1881.

HORACE—GARFIELD.

HORACE is said to have been a great favorite of the lamented Garfield. A day or two since, a scholar, fresh from the reading of the Thirtieth Ode of the Third Book, wherein the poet, a privileged egotist, confidently predicts the perpetuity of his own fame (in his case remarkably verified), thought it strange that no one had noticed the peculiar applicableness of the verses to the late President. That they do admit of an easy application, to some extent, at least, is indeed quite manifest, of which the explanation is to be found in the striking similarity of the lots of the two men. Horace speaks of himself elsewhere as the child of poor parents, "*pauperum sanguis parentum,*" and here as having risen to eminence from a mean estate, "*ex humili potens;*" and so after he had become the intimate associate and bosom friend of the first men of Rome, and in high favor with Augustus himself, he took no pains to conceal the fact of his humble birth. He was noted for his vigorous common sense and his consummate mastery of expression. The parallel thus far is exact. But Horace was a pagan and not a Christian. The only immortality he knew was an earthly immortality, to be derived from his writings. Those words of the sixth line of the ode, so powerful in their brevity, and which are so much more significant in the mouth of a Christian believer, would form an appropriate inscription for the tomb yet to be erected to Garfield:

Non Omnis Moriar!

CARMEN XXX.
LIBER III.

Exegi monumentum ære perennius
Regalique situ pyramidum altius;
Quod non imber edax, non Aquilo impotens
Possit diruere, aut innumerabilis
Annorum series, et fuga temporum.
Non omnis moriar! multaque pars mei
Vitabit Libitinam. Usque ego postera
Crescam laude recens, dum Capitolium
Scandet cum tacita Virgine pontifex.
Dicar, qua violens obstrepit Aufidus,*

---

*Now Ofanto in Apulia. Horace was born on its banks. Daunus, a legendary king, ruled over the southern part of Apulia, as the Aufidus flowed through the western.

Et qua pauper aquæ Daunus agrestium
Regnavit populorum, ex humili potens,
Princeps Æolium carmen ad Italos
Deduxisse modos. Sume superbiam
Quæsitam meritis, et mihi Delphica
Lauro cinge volens, Melpomene, comam.

A NEW TRANSLATION.

I've reared a monument alone
More durable than brass or stone;
Whose cloudy summit is more hid
Than regal height of pyramid;
Which rains that beat and winds that blow
Shall not have power to overthrow,
Nor countless years that silent smite,
Nor seasons in their onward flight.
I will not, when I yield my breath,
Die wholly! much escaping death,
I will increase, my fame shall grow,
Be fresh in aftertimes as now,
And while the silent vestal shall
Climb with the priest the Capitol,

I—risen from a low estate
To be both powerful and great,
Where rushing Aufidus complains
And Daunus o'er parched regions reigns—
Shall be declared and honored long
As one who first the stream of song
Led down from its Æolic head,
To run in an Italian bed.
Put on that pride, Melpomene,
By merit so befitting thee,
To me propitious be alway,
And bind my hair with Delphic bay!

SEPTEMBER 28, 1881.

TRANSLATIONS OF HORACE.

THE first of the two following Odes of Horace is characterized by unusual vivacity and verve. In liveliness of fancy and lyric abandon, it is surpassed by nothing the author has written. The poets, instead of dying and being buried like ordinary mortals, allegorically represented themselves as transformed into swans.

ix

This pleasant conceit is here egotistically expanded by the poet-prophet into a confident prediction of his future fame. The other Ode, addressed to Virgil, is a Tennysonian "In Memoriam" or dirge on the death of Quintilius Varus, a mutual friend.

Book II.—Carmen XX.

Ad Mæcenatem.

Non usitata, nec tenui ferar
Penna biformis per liquidum æthera
   Vates: neque in terris morabor
     Longius; invidiaque major

Urbes relinquam. Non ego pauperum
Sanguis parentum, non ego, quem vocas
   Dilecte, Mæcenas, obibo,
     Nec Stygia cohibebor unda.

Jam jam residunt cruribus asperæ
Pelles; et album mutor in alitem
   Superna; nascunturque leves
     Per digitos humerosque plumæ.

Jam Dædaleo notior Icaro
Visam gementis litora Bospori,
   Syrtesque Gætulas canorus
      Ales Hyperboreosque campos.

Me Colchus, et qui dissimulat metum
Marsæ cohortis, Dacus, et ultimi
   Noscent Geloni: me peritus
      Discet Iber, Rhodanique potor.

Absint iani funere næniæ,
Luctusque turpes et querimoniæ:
   Compesce clamorem, ac sepulcri
      Mitte supervacuos honores.

Translation.

To Mæcenas.

I will soar on a pinion of excellent might,
  By the right of a power on poets conferred,
Through the clear realms of ether will take my far
     flight
  In my duplicate shape of a bard and a bird,

No longer on earth will I draw out my stay,
　I envy will leave and the cities behind.
Though of poor parents born, while Mæcenas shall say
　I'm his friend, I'll not die, nor by Styx be confined.

Now, now, a rough skin my thighs settles on,
　From my fingers and shoulders spring feathers of down;
I'm changed to a bird, all white, like the swan,
　A bird of the fairest and grandest renown.

Than Icarus more swift, I will visit the lands
　Where the Euxine is making perpetual moan
And fields Hyperborean and African sands,
　Still a bird sweetly warbling in various tone.

Me the Colchians shall know, and the Dacian, his fear
　Of the Marcian cohorts dissembling, shall own;
Me the far-away Scythians will learn to revere,
　Me the Spaniard, and he, too, who drinks of the Rhone.

Since empty the urn, let no dirges be said,
　No groans let there be, no funereal gloom,
Be clamor all hushed, and let there be paid
　No superfluous honors when naught 's in the tomb.

Book I.—Carmen XXIV.

Ad Virgilium.

Quis desiderio sit pudor aut modus
Tam cari capitis? ͵Præcipe lugubres
Cantus, Melpomene, cui liquidam Pater
   Vocem cum cithara dedit.

Ergo Quintilium perpetuus sopor
Urget! cui Pudor, et Justitiæ soror,
Incorrupta Fides, nudaque Veritas
   Quando ullum inveniet parem?

Multis ille bonis flebilis occidit;
Nulli flebilior, quam tibi, Virgili.
Tu frustra pius, heu! non ita creditum
   Poscis Quintilium deos.

Quod si Threicio blandius Orpheo
Auditam moderere arboribus fidem,
Non vanæ redeat sanguis imagini,
   Quam virga semel horrida,

Non lenis precibus fata recludere,
Nigro compulerit Mercurius gregi.
Durum! Sed levius fit patientia,
   Quidquid corrigere est nefas.

Translation.

To Virgil.

To love and grief o'erhead so dear,
    What shame or limit can there be?
    Lead the lament, Melpomene,
With lyre and voice resounding clear!

Since fetters now Quintilius bind,
    Fetters of endless sleep, ah, when
    Shall Modesty, Faith tried of men,
And naked Truth his equal find?

By many good men wept he died,
    By none more, Virgil, than by thee.
    Him back thou asked'st fruitlessly,
Thy pious prayers the gods denied.

Not if thou sway'dst a lyre, more bland
    Than his which charmed the listening wood,
    Back to that shade ne'er comes the blood
Whom Hermes with his horrid wand,

Inexorable and deaf to prayer,
    With his dark flock folds once for all.
    But Patience, let what will befall,
Lightens the load and helps to bear.

JANUARY, 1882.

PARIS IN 1848 AND 1871.

A PERSONAL EXPERIENCE.

EIGHTEEN hundred and forty-eight, it will be remembered, was a year fertile of revolutions. I sailed for Europe early in February. Previous to my leaving, nobody seemed to be aware that a great crisis was impending. A fishing smack which came alongside of our vessel when we arrived off Land's End, first brought us the news of the events of the three days of February —the flight of Louis Philippe, the downfall of the French Monarchy, and the establishment of a Republic in its stead. At first we were most incredulous, and disposed to set it down as one of the biggest "yarns." It was not to be credited, we thought, that he who was reported to be the wisest, the most sagacious and politic of the reigning sovereigns, who had neglected no means to strengthen and establish his throne, could be displaced so easily, and with circumstances of so much degradation, as if he had been some casual, rascally intruder, who had got clandestine access to the seat of royalty, and been turned out as soon as discovered. Nevertheless, it was even so; and the extraordinary events there in France, were the signal of other events, which were quickly to follow, not less extraordinary, in neighboring countries. Democracy everywhere became rampant. The new power swept on with the impetuosity of a whirlwind, prostrating all before it. Abrupt, startling, like the fall of a thunderbolt, or the concussion of an earthquake, was the explosion of the popular element. A little leaven leaveneth the whole lump. No sooner had the tocsin of the French Revolution sounded, than quick as thought, simultaneous as sympathy, spontaneous as instinct, the dear hope of liberty, slumbering in unnumbered hearts, awoke; and everywhere men became electrically excited and dangerous with passion. As if they had read the handwriting on the walls of their palaces, and knew they were doomed of heaven, kings and rulers yielded at once with hardly a show of resistance. Like a thief surprised in the midst of his plunder, they hastened to restore to the people those rights of which they had been so long deprived.

In some cases, to be sure, a little reluctance was manifested; but in others the readiness was extreme;

and the offer of restitution almost anticipated the demand. The small States in the South-West of Germany, as being neighboring and nearest, first arose. Baden, Hesse-Cassel, Wurtemburg, Bavaria, Nassau, Frankfort, Saxony, Saxe-Weimar and more besides, burst out one after the other, and in quick succession, into revolutionary flame. They demanded Constitutions, which should guarantee to them freedom of the press, trial by jury, equal rights, equality of all before the law, universal suffrage, and such like; and no Duke, Elector or King had the boldness to refuse. Prussia and Austria soon followed.

But before this, so rapid was the course of events, the initiative had already been taken, and considerable progress had been made towards a consummation, which had long formed the subject of devout desire to political dreamers and enthusiasts. Old Germania, long passed away, mouldering in the grave of centuries, was destined they had believed, nevertheless, to have one day a glorious resurrection. Everything justified the hope that that day was near, was now. What moment so auspicious as the present, a present teeming with miracles, to raise the dead! To bring about a revival of German nationality; to take out of the way all the artificial barriers and partitions which had served to divide and keep asunder what was so naturally and properly one; to realize, in a word, the great idea of German unity, was an object dear to the German heart, and gave birth to the German Parliament meeting at Frankfort.

After a while came what was called "reactions," *attroupements*, internecine feuds, alternate successes and reverses, a crowd of events extraordinary, beyond precedent, followed close upon one another, as wave follows wave. In France, the Provisional Government, with Lamartine, the poet-statesman, at its head, after a brief and uneasy existence of less than four months, set in blood. Quitting London, where I had made a short stay and witnessed a Chartist uprising formidable enough to require the aid of a Wellington to put down, I crossed the channel, and arrived in Paris some time in April, and was an eye-witness of the exciting scenes that preceded the terrible outbreak in June. While it might be claiming too much to say, *quorum pars magna fui*, I saw, at least, the Insurrection, if I did not share in it, from the beginning to the end. I was present, as it so happened, at the building of the first barricade, and had extraordinary opportunities throughout for a near observation of all that took place at that memorable epoch.

I had watched and waited for the catastrophe, knew that it was impending and inevitable, sometime before it arrived. Then, as now, shut up in Paris, were the representatives of two great parties. The party in power, made up of moderates, were sincere Republicans, with notions of liberty, a little sentimental and Frenchy perhaps, but tolerably just and reasonable, who labored with honest earnestness to organize a government calculated to secure it. The other party, consisting mostly of the "baser sort," ignorant and unprincipled, calling themselves workmen (*ouvriers*), but the majority of them the most idle and vicious of the class, mixed up, it may be, with some well-meaning and misguided persons—organized into clubs, and incited by bad and designing men, soon began to dictate and to threaten, with boundless insolence, dangerous to the tottering and unsettled foundations of the existing government. The expected collision at last came; and after a doubtful and bloody struggle, the Reds were defeated. Martial law was declared, and Lamartine with his associates, scientists, poets, publicists—at best theoretic statesmen—gave place to the soldier, Cavaignac, and France underwent another of those "transformations" to which, according to Victor Hugo, she is so much addicted. An election was ordered, and before the close of that most eventful year, Louis Napoleon was chosen President of the French Republic, by a majority so overwhelming as to make it doubtful even then, whether Bonapartism had not usurped the place of Republicanism in the heart of the nation. About the same time, the King of Prussia promulged a constitution of his own devising, dissolving at the same time, most arbitrarily, the Constitutional Assembly, to whom the task of preparing it had been committed; the Emperor of Austria abdicated in favor of his nephew; and the Pope fled in disguise from his dominions. After three years came the *coup d'etat* of Louis Napoleon — thenceforth Napoleon III.*

* * * * * * *

Admitting that the real cause of the present war between France and Germany was other than the ostensible one, and that the true motive was national jealousy looking for a pretext, the fact remains, that none could be found but one more frivolous even than that which

> "Launched a thousand ships
> And burnt the topless towers of Ilium;"

* See "The Microcosm and Other Poems," p. 161.

and out of it have come more than an "Iliad of woes." We sit at home by our pleasant firesides, and languidly read prosaic telegrams of yesterday's battles, compared with which those fought on the plains of ancient Troy, forming the subject matter of Homer's immortal Epic, were petty and bloodless.

* * * * * * *

Let Prussia beware, lest in the end her victory prove a Cadmean victory, one in which she will suffer as much as her enemy. Bacon relates of Henry VII, that he always professed to love and seek Peace, and that his usual preface in his treaties, was: "When Christ came into the world, Peace was sung, and when He went out Peace was bequeathed!" It is to be hoped that the newly-declared Emperor of Germany will act in the spirit of so divine a sentiment, and not protract the war a single hour beyond what is necessary. Let him remember, Emperor though he be,

"And though his arm should conquer twenty worlds,
There is a lean fellow that beats all conquerors,"

and that he too, and that right soon, must answer at

the judgment bar of the Most High God, for all the deeds done in the body.

In closing this review of a period going back twenty-three years, during which it is safe to say, what with wars in the Crimea, in India, in Italy, in America, in Germany, and now again in France, there has been an amount of bloodshed unmatched in the history of the world, it is natural to enquire whether anything has been gained by all this dreadful waste in brief mortality. Something, we would fain hope, to the cause of civil liberty. In Italy, national unity is *un fait accompli*, with an indefinite enlargement of the domain of freedom. In Austria and in Spain there has been a wonderful advance. At home we are happily freed from the incubus of slavery. Serfdom has been abolished in Russia. All this would seem to indicate progress. Everything human, however, is imperfect. All governments hitherto have been little better than attempts at government. Those governments deemed the strongest, have been found when tested, utter weakness, and passed away in an hour. What are armies and navies and munitions of war but signs of weakness—the props and supports of a falling edifice? We are probably destined to witness this strange and shifting phantasmagoria of vanishing thrones, of shams and semblances, of would-bes and are-nots, until that kingdom which is said to come "without observation," and to be ."within" us, and whose characteristic is "forever," is fully set up.

NEWARK, 1871.

ROME, ITALY.

FEBRUARY, 1854.

ONE chief charm of this melancholy city just now is its foreign society; and the English and American visitors far outnumber all others. An observing friend, who is curious in statistics, reckons the number at seventeen hundred; and they seem, for the most part disposed to be as agreeable as possible, individual and home distinctions being for the time merged in a more generous feeling of fellowship. So that one may sometimes see "lords and ladies" by courtesy mingling without insolence in the same circles with our untitled American noblesse—possessing, indeed, honorably acquired patents to social recognition abroad, though inferior, it may be, in that self-discipline, that ease and simplicity of manner which is among the latest results of refinement and cultivation in polite intercourse. In truth, that easy and becoming air which Tully celebrates as the distinguishing mark of an accomplished gentleman, is a rare attainment anywhere. But, after all, the great charm of intelligent social intercourse is breadth of sympathy, and I know of no pleasanter refreshment after a fatiguing day among these stupendous remains of ancient ostentation, than an American reunion at one of *Mrs. Crawford's* agreeable soirees,* where Truth and Nature keep company with the Graces. The society of Rome itself is more ostentatious and less cheerful than that of either of the other Italian capitals. In fact, few of the noble families open their doors for company. The habitual gloom which hangs over the city, affects also the social atmosphere. * * * *

The Coliseum is a striking image of the city itself—decayed, vacant, gloomy, half gray and half green, erect

---

* Those of the Hon. and Mrs. Wm. B. Kinney, in Florence, Dr. Coles found to be equally agreeable and entertaining; there he met Robert and Elizabeth Barrett Browning and others of literary fame.

While in Florence, Dr. Coles was also a welcome guest at the home and studio of Hiram Powers. The marble busts of "Eve" and "Charity," by this distinguished American sculptor, were subsequently purchased by Dr. Coles and are now at Deerhurst.

on one side and fallen on the other, with consecrated ground in the middle; visited withal by people of all sorts, moralists, antiquaries, artists, devotees, etc. The emptiness and stillness of the streets contrast painfully with those of living cities, though this is in keeping with the desolate majesty of the city of the Cæsars. The sound of carts and carriages is rarely heard, and after nine in the evening profound stillness reigns. * * *

—From "*Correspondence of the Newark Daily Advertiser.*"

WINDERMERE.*

ONCE more, sweet Windermere! once more
    I tread thy consecrated shore:
From distant lands my pilgrim feet
Have sought thy exquisite retreat,
Where thou, like holiest anchorite,
Dost muse by day and dream by night,
While mirrored in thy peaceful breast,
All images of beauty rest—

---

*Westmoreland, England. Wordsworth, Southey, Coleridge, Wilson (Christopher North), De Quincey, etc., were all sometime residents of the Lake District.

The glories of the morn and even,
The matchless excellence of heaven.

The mountains, towering and grand,
O'erlooking thee, enamored stand;
Well pleased, each in his proper place
To catch new glimpses of thy face.
With what a splendor God endows
Their most superb and kingly brows!
Yet not the proudest far or near,
But holds thee honorable and dear.
How those behind would seem to strain,
And tiptoe stand a sight to gain!

A higher homage yet than these
Is whispered in the passing breeze;
Celestial warblings, soft and clear,
Steal sweetly on my ravished ear.
O favored Lake! above whose banks,
Immortal Bards have sung their thanks,
For that they knew to thee they owed
Much of the rapture they bestowed,
That half the secret of their art
Was thy shrined beauty in their heart.

1855.

NIAGARA.*

FOREVERMORE, from thee, Niagara!
    Religious Cataract! Most Holy Fane!
A service and a symphony go up
Into the ear of God. 'Tis Sabbath morn.
My soul, refreshed and full of comfort, hears
Thy welcome call to worship. All night long
A murmur, like the memory of a sound,
Has filled my sleep and made my dreams devout.
It was the deep unintermittent roll
Of thy eternal anthem, pealing still
Upon the slumbering and muffled sense,
Thence echoing in the soul's mysterious depths
With soft reverberations. How the earth
Trembles with hallelujahs, loud as break
From banded Seraphim and Cherubim
Singing before the Throne, while God vouchsafes
Vision and audience to prostrate Heaven!
My soul, that else were mute, transported finds
In you, O inarticulate Harmonies!

*From the poem, "A Sabbath at Niagara."

Expression for unutterable thoughts,
Surpassing the impertinence of words.
For that the petty artifice of speech
Cannot pronounce th' Unpronounceable,
Nor meet the infinite demands of praise
Before descending Godhead, lo! she makes
Of this immense significance of sound,
Sublime appropriation, chanting it anew,
As her "Te Deum," and sweet Hymn of Laud.

THE BETTER COUNTRY.

BERNARD OF CLUNY (12TH CENTURY).

TRANSLATION.

THE last of the hours, iniquity towers,
   The times are the worst, let us vigils be keeping!
Lest the Judge who is near, and soon to appear,
   Shall us at His coming find slumbering and sleeping.
He is nigh, He is nigh! He descends from the sky
   For the ending of evil, the right's coronation,
The just to reward, relief to afford,
   And the heavens bestow for the saints' habitation:

To lift and unbind grievous weights from the mind,
   To give every man what is just and is equal,
To make the good glad, and punish the bad,
   To the praise of His justice and grace in the sequel.
Most clement and dear, most just and severe,
   Lo! cometh the King in terrible splendor,
Man springs from the sod, and the Man who is God,
   The Judge from the Father, stands sentence to render.

    *   *   *   *   *   *   *

The life here below so brief is brief woe,
   A brief mortal space for weeping afforded;—
Not briefly to sigh, then lie down and die,
   Is the life that 's to be hereafter awarded.
O most blessèd award! the gift of the Lord,
   A life whose long years cannot be computed;
O strange award given! a mansion in heaven
   Assigned to the guilty, the sometime polluted.
What 's given, and to whom? In the firmament, room
   To the needy and those by the cross worthy rendered—
Yea, on Mercy's sweet terms, orbs celestial to worms,
   To felons the best, to the hateful stars, tendered.
Now are battles most hard; after these the reward.

Reward of what sort? Reward without measure;—
Full refreshment, repose, full exemption from woes,
  No suffering, no pain, only unalloyed pleasure.
Now live we in hope, and Zion must cope
  With Babylon proud and the powers infernal;
Now affliction makes sad, then delight shall make glad,
  And there shall be crowns and sceptres supernal.
Then new glory divine on the righteous shall shine,
  And chase from their breasts the darkness that paineth,
Chase doubt and chase fear, and enigmas make clear—
  The light of true sabbaths, "the rest that remaineth."
All free from the foe and his master shall go,
  The Hebrew, whose feet heavy chains now environ,—
He henceforth held free shall keep jubilee,
  No more to be bound in affliction and iron.
A Country of light, unacquainted with night,
  Where of tempest and strife nothing breaks the deep slumber,
With inhabitants free it replenished shall be—
  Enlarged with true Israelites countless in number.

Country splendid and grand, and a flowery land
  That's free from all thorns and free from all
    dangers,
Is there to be given to the free born of heaven—
  The faithful, who here are now pilgrims and
    strangers.
Shall then be unrolled, to all that behold
  The face of the Thunderer, and to such solely,
The utmost extreme of power supreme,
  Full knowledge, the unutterable peace of the holy:
A peace by the tongue of slander unstung;
  A peace without storm, without wrangling or rancor,
To labors a goal, and to billows that roll
  And tumults a fixed immovable anchor.
My King is my part, God Himself in my heart,
  In His own proper beauty august and endearing
I shall see and enshrine and challenge as mine,—
  My Author and Saviour,—before Him appearing.
Then the Israel of grace shall Jacob displace,
  And Leah be Rachel in form and affection;
Then Zion shall stand, a beautiful land,
  In all the completeness of God-like perfection.
O Country most dear, our longing eyes here,
  As they view thee afar, with desire are aching;

At the sound of thy name our hearts are aflame,
  And our eyes are aweary 'twixt weeping and
    waking.
Thy mention brings rest, is balm to the breast,
  Is the cure of our grief, and takes away sadness;
The thinking of thee and the bliss that shall be,
  Is a fire of love and a fountain of gladness.
The only place thou that draws our hearts now,—
  Thou Paradise art, thou our blissful Hereafter;
No tears are found there, no sorrow, no care,
  But serenest rejoicings and innocent laughter.
There planted are seen, eternally green,
  The laurel and cedar, with the hyssop low growing;
There are walls with the rays of the jasper ablaze,
  With the carbuncle bright, incandescent and glow-
    ing:
The sardius shines there, here the topaz most rare,
  Here the beams of the amethyst with the rest
    mingle;
To thy fabric belong the heavenly throng,
  The corner-stone Christ, gem precious and single.
Without shore, without time, everlasting sublime,
  Thou, fountain and stream late hitherward flowing,
To the good tastest sweet, living rock at their feet

That all through the wilderness gladdened their going.
Thine 's the laurel's green crown with its leaf never brown;
Rich dower all golden, fair spouse, is thee given;
Thine 's the exquisite bliss of the Prince's first kiss,
And the sight of His face like a vision of heaven.
Fair lilies and white, living gems flashing bright,
Compose, happy spouse, thy bridal adorning;
Sits the Lamb by thy side, and beams on His bride,
Like the sun when he breaks through the gates of the morning;
Thy whole sweet employ, in triumph and joy,
Sweet anthems of praise to warble forever;
Evils merited tell, blessings granted as well,
With shoutings to grace that terminate never.
City golden and blest, from thy fields' teeming breast
Flow rivers of milk,—fair people, fair dwellings;
Thou the whole heart dost whelm, such the charms of thy realm,
Choked is the voice with the heart's mighty swellings.
Confined here below, I pretend not to know
What forms this rejoicing, the kind of light given,

Nor how lofty the heights of those social delights,
  Nor how special the glory that constitutes heaven.
These striving to raise in an effort of praise,
  My mind overmastered, lo! fainteth and faileth;
O glory unknown, I am conquered I own,
  Thy superior praise in all things prevaileth.
There are shoutings and calls in thy echoing halls
  With the martyr host full, a glorious muster,
With the citizen, bright, with the Prince aye in sight,
  Serene evermore with a soft, sacred lustre.
There sweet pastures around for the gentle abound,
  For the saints a dear flock by the water brooks grazing;
There's the throne of the King, there the palace-walls ring
  With the sound of a multitude feasting and praising.
Nation glorious and grand, through the conquering hand
  Of the Leader, a host in white vestments shining,
Through the long rolling years they remain without tears;
  In the dwellings of Zion there is rest from repining.
Without crime, without storm, to mar and deform,
  Without weapons of strife, without matter of quarrel,

THE BETTER COUNTRY.

The Israelites blest in their lofty homes rest,—
  The olive of peace intertwined with the laurel.
O illustrious name, Zion, highest in fame,
  Whose glory is that to the glorified owing,
Thou dost knowledge dispense to the innermost sense,
  Thy innermost good thus secretly showing.
My innermost eyes, thus piercing the skies,
  From the mind's highest peaks delighted behold thee;
Now my breast, all on fire with hope and desire,
  Transported expects sometime to enfold thee.
Thou Zion art one, beside thee is none,—
  Upreared in the skies a mythical dwelling,—
Now in thee I am glad, now in me I am sad,
  I sob and I sigh with breast heaving and swelling.
Since the body's dull clod keeps me back from my God,
  Thee to pierce I oft try with spiritual pinion,
But earthy flesh, fleshy earth, makes th' attempt little worth,
  And I quickly fall back to the senses' dominion.
No mortal may dare with his mouth to declare—
  The talk were presumptuous and desperate the duty—

Where thy walls, how they rise, in what part of the skies
　Thy capitals shine complete in their beauty.
Thy charms, they weigh down the heart wholly and drown,
　O Zion! O Peace beyond all conceiving!
City blest, without time, dear, tranquil, sublime,
　No possible praise can e'er be deceiving.
No delights vain and lewd, and no sorrows intrude,
　No strife with its wasting, its burning and blasting;
Home happy and high, flowery land of the sky,
　Land native to bliss and the life everlasting.
City, seen from afar, where the glorified are,
　On a safe and high shore, lo! thy towers are soaring,
Thee I sue, I admire, thee I love, I desire,
　Sing hymns unto thee, and salute thee adoring.
Not on merit, but grace, I rest solely my case,
　For, measured by merit, condemned my condition;
Not dumb and perverse do I cover the worse—
　I own I 'm a child of wrath and perdition.
My life 's a life spilt, void of good, full of guilt,
　A life like to death, without vital expressions,
Its innocence quenched, from its proper life wrenched,

Destroyed by reason of deadly transgressions.
Notwithstanding in hope I walk softly and grope,
  In hope and in faith heavenly guerdons beseeching;
I trembling and weak, eternal joys seek,
  By night and by day imploring hands reaching.
Our Father above, whose nature is love,
  The best and the dearest, He made and He saved me,
With my vileness He bore, from my vileness He tore,
  From my sin and uncleanness He graciously laved me.
Grace celestial alone, direct from the throne,*
  Is the sovereign provision of God's own appointing,
The sordid of soul to save and make whole,
  For inward diseases the potent anointing.
Grace washes away all pollution for aye,—
  The Fountain of David, as free as redundant,
Makes pure all within, makes clean from all sin,
  To all alike flows in measure abundant.
O excellent grace! to an excellent place
  Me raise to discern stately palaces gleaming,
At a distance, at least, see the heavenly feast,
  With holiest mirth and melody teeming.

  *Grace celestial alone is the only means known. First edition.

THE BETTER COUNTRY.

Thou Zion! O mine, my hope all divine!
   Like gold, but far nobler, t' our dazzled eyes
      looming,
Most brilliant thy host, but their Leader 's thy boast,
   Brave region with laurel perpetually blooming.
O Country most sweet, shall my eyes ever greet
   Thy turrets and towers, and know thy enjoyments?
O Country most blessed, e'er in thee shall I rest,
   Possess thy rewards and share thy employments?
Tell me, I pray, render answer, and say:
   "Thou shalt hereafter most surely behold me—
I hope entertain, the thing hoped shall I gain?*
   O say: Thou forever shalt have, and shalt hold me.†
Advanced to that sphere, O holy, most dear,
   O blessèd, thrice blessèd and blessèd forever,
Who with cleaving of heart, chose God for his part:
   O wretched, undone, who from this did him sever.

      —*From "Old Gems in New Settings."*

---

  * I solid hope grasp, what I hope shall I clasp? First edition.
  † O say: In thy arms thou forever shalt hold me. First edition.

PROEM.

[FROM "THE EVANGEL."*]

SPIRIT DIVINE, the adding up of gifts,
    Communicable Godhead, be my Guest!
Grant me the true afflatus that uplifts,
    And be the oracle within my breast!
Guide me into all truth! bestow Thy best—
    Life, light, and love, that clarity of being
Without which there can be no certainty of seeing,

    No right discernment, singleness of eye!
    In vain Thy beams illuminate the page:
    In vain the azure of that blessed sky
    Blazons dear attributes from age to age:
    Blinded philosopher, and darkling sage,
    The wise and prudent, seeing, nothing see,
Because there dwells in them no true sincerity.

---

*Among letters received by Dr. Coles, in which mention is made of "The Evangel" and "The Light of the World," we find one from the Right Hon. W. E. Gladstone, M. P., written from 10 Downing street, Whitehall, January 17, 1885; and one from Stephen Gladstone, written from Hawarden Rectory, Chester, February 20, 1885.

O ignorance and folly of the wise!
Men never tire of endless labor, spent
In building Babels, and in babbling lies;
Blowing up bubbles of most gay ostent,
Mere emptiness, on solemn trifling bent:
They from creation the Creator take,
And then th' astonished air with their Eurekas shake.

Of that called Science, much is only guess.
False as the Koran half that it declares:
It feigns beginnings full of foolishness—*
Faith hath its ladder which it climbs by prayers—
This jumps the moon in fault of facts for stairs;
And Ignorance, that cannot make a pin,
Will make you myriad worlds, and throw as many in.

Science is certainty, is truth found out,
Not dreams about the genesis of man,
Monstrous assumings, that admit no doubt
He from the lowest forms of life began.
We dare to call him cheat and charlatan,
Pretender, and no architect at all,
Who builds on airy guess a leaning, tottering wall.

* See Dr. Coles' criticism in "The Evangel," pp. 4-12, on Mr. Darwin's work, "The Descent of Man."

A specious likelihood helps not the case;
One single proof were worth a million such:
Science is never broader than its base;
Th' extended fabric topples at a touch,
Jutting o'er fact—a hair's breadth is too much—
For there is emptiness and the abyss,
Hungry for unrealities as vain as this.

It is the greater that includes the less,
Not less the greater. One is not made four
But by addition. From all singleness
Th' involved unit is evolved, no more—
Development increases not the store—
After its kind each thing unfolds its powers:
Man sums and tops them all—and by *addition* towers

Not *evolution;* otherwise he ought,
When dormant in the mollusk, to have woke,
Growing to more till to perfection brought,
Seen to be nearer as each morning broke—
As from the acorn grows unstayed the oak—
In straight progression to his goal and bound:
Not mollusk after mollusk circling round and round,

Through all the ages not advanced a jot.
Which is he, then, philosopher or fool?
Who gropes in protoplasm and finds a dot,
And calls it man, according to the school,
Far famed, of whittlers, whittling down by rule
Humanity, till of humanity bereft,
A microscopic cypher, meaning naught, is left:

And then, lest this primordial cell should hold
Reason for Deity, they it invert
And spill the life; and of the mighty old
Nothing retain, but simply dregs and dirt—
Matter and force—whence rose, they dare assert,
A Godless universe: blind struggle and endeavor
Securing God-like ends infallibly forever.

Since they deny not to the world we see
Birth and beginning, and are proud to show
Their learned aptness in cosmogony—
How vulgar dust became, we seek to know,
Germ of the Infinite, God in embryo,
Where hidden lay not only heaven and earth,
But waiting Deity Himself, not come to birth.

Omniscience is somewhere: we must assume
Omniscient atom, or omniscient mind—
A boundless Unit in unbounded room—
An All in all, or under or behind—
Or God, or His equivalent, that designed
After ideals this majestic whole,
And gave to man a moral and religious soul.

Justice there is, administrative Right,
Somewhere, in something, name it as you may,
Wielding a sceptre of imperial might,
Whose awful mandates none may disobey:
"You ought, you shall, you must," we hear it say:
The voice is God's, unless the voice deceive,
And we in high judicial atoms can believe.

If Nature does not juggle us, we are;
Not only are, but are the thing we seem—
No docetism of science, making jar
'Twixt fact and fact, convinces us we dream:
They sin against their Maker and blaspheme
Who trust the lower and distrust the higher,
And criminating consciousness make God a liar.

Mind is and rules, and matter is her slave—
Resistless might and monarchy of will
Over wide realms a thousand sceptres wave,
Making blind force her purposes fulfill—
Supreme in freedom, knowing good and ill:
Th' accountable I am, the moral me,
By no dissolving bands is joined to Deity.

Knowledge is good, divine it is to know—
Man's earliest instinct is a cry for light.
O for some guiding certainty below!
For full of doubt and terror is the night
Vague threatening shapes the guilty soul affright:
Reason and conscience sound alarms within,
And tremble at the possibilities of sin.

Divine Evangel, from four trumpets blown,
Filled with melodious and immortal breath,
To all the world forgiveness making known,
And free salvation from eternal death!
O, hearken the glad news it witnesseth,
Ye sons of men, beware how you despise
The voice of your Redeemer speaking from the skies.

"IN THE BEGINNING WAS THE WORD (THE LOGOS), AND THE WORD WAS WITH GOD, AND THE WORD WAS GOD."

[JOHN I: 1.]

THE first Christians, the unlearned particularly, implicitly received and worshipped Christ as God. Theirs was *the intuitive view*, the faith of children. But many of the early Christians, Justin Martyr and others, were *Platonists* before they were Christians. Plato lived four hundred years before Christ. Philo, an Alexandrian Jew, contemporary with the apostles, set the example of tracing out pagan analogies—seeking the germs of the Greek philosophy in the Jewish Scriptures, and finding Plato in Moses. The easy adaptation of the theosophic speculations of the one concerning the Logos or Divine Reason, to the inspired disclosures of the other concerning Jehovah and the Word of Jehovah; with the personification of Wisdom met with in Proverbs VIII. and elsewhere, would favor minglings leading to corruptions of the Divine testimony, and furnish occasion to the last of the Evangelists, in this sublime Prologue to his Gospel, to assert the true doctrine of the Logos, separated from that which was false, introduced by the earlier and later Platonizers and Gnostics.

In the sects that early sprung up it is easy to trace the corrupting influence of Judaism and heathen philosophy. While the *Ebionites*, half Jews, denied, like our modern Unitarians, the divinity of Christ; the *Gnostics*, half heathen, denied in various ways His humanity.

* * * * * * *

The Reformed Churches, in making up their Confessions of Faith, distinctly rejected and condemned Arianism, Ebionism, Marcionism (Docetic Gnosticism), Sabellianism, Apollinarianism, Nestorianism, Eutychianism and Monothelitism or Monophysitism as well as the Lutheran doctrine of the ubiquity of Christ's body.

* * * * * * *

"Whom do men say that I, the Son of Man, am?" To this question of our Lord we have had in the Creeds, Confessions and Christologies, variant and warring of earlier and later times, the manifold answer. "But whom do ye, my disciples, say that I am?" The appeal is from the wise to the simple. In the hush of loud theologies let experience speak. First of all then, and above all, Christ is to the believer the revelation of a need. He is certified as divine, inasmuch as a Saviour less than divine were no Saviour at all, because unequal to the felt necessity of a help miraculous and infinite: for, in justifying man, God must justify Himself. What miracle so stupendous as the Divine inconsistency of a judicial reversal of a just sentence! Who reconciles warring attributes and self-contradictions of Godhead; terminates the law without repealing it; magnifies it when broken by pardon in lieu of penalty; condemns the sin and saves the sinner; does more than create—mirrors, one might say, the transcendent effulgence of an impossible Omnipotence. This is the work ascribed to Christ throughout the New Testament. His divinity is not a matter of texts, but texture. It forms the very warp and woof of the whole fabric. That He does not condescend to the vulgar egotism of a perpetual self-assertion, befits Him; but every where and always He is seen to be God in action—exercising divine prerogatives; stilling tempests and forgiving sins; healing the sick and raising the dead—all with the quiet ease and composed majesty of One unconscious of doing any thing extraordinary: and, finally, laying down His life and taking it again, He ascends on high to resume the glory which He had with the Father before the world was.

One is tempted to wonder at the presumption of men who, profoundly ignorant of their own nature, dare to dogmatize concerning God's; and annex an Athanasian *Quicunque vult* (Whoever would be saved) to each formulated affirmation and finding contained in their creed. A doctrine and the definition of a doctrine are very different things. It is quite possible, therefore, to believe in the doctrine and not the definition. Any definition of an infinite subject must of necessity be incomplete. It can only include a part and not the whole. The moment we begin to define Godhead our difficulties begin. What is hard to the defining intellect is easy to faith.

We are liable, doubtless, to do great injustice to another's view of a many-sided truth, by not seeing what he sees at his angle of vision.

* * * * * * *

We are saved by Faith rather than a Creed: because Faith is a divine gift; a great, vital fact of human experience, having its birth and beginning in the profoundest depths of the renewed heart: whereas a Creed is more an affair of the intellect; an invented symbol or mould of doctrine, into which are cast—as the name "Symbol," the synonym of Creed, implies—the gathered result of the severe questionings of the controversial crucible, the divine gold, as it passes out of the fire, still debased, alas! with the inevitable alloy of human passion and speculation. The difference between truth in the intellect and in the heart is that of plants stored in a *hortus siccus*, and the same, blooming and breathing fragrance in the growing Garden of the Lord.

The lesson to be deduced from this review is one of charity. "Judge not lest ye be judged." Not but that a right creed is supremely important. All error is quicksand, and dangerous to build upon. But humility is of the ground and takes hold of the rock. Better were it if, discarding pride, men could be content to leave the mysteries of the Godhead where Revelation leaves them: to stop where it stops. God is a unit, but a unit understood by none. The Trinity is a dear and divine fact, not explained because unexplainable. It belongs not to arithmetic. Arithmetic adds and subtracts, but the Infinite admits of neither subtraction nor addition. It is enough to know that "God is *in* Christ, reconciling the world to Himself, not imputing to men their trespasses;" and that this paradox of grace has its deep origin in the Triune paradox of a God, at once sole and social, happy from all eternity in the ineffable endearments and communings of a plural and loving Oneness—God in God, with God, from God—sweetly distinguished as the Father, the Son, and the Proceeding Spirit. Who would exchange the exhilarations of belief in such a proclaimed EVANGEL, for the dreary negations of doubt, and the resultant horror of atheistic despair!

THY SERVANTS OF THE PEN.

HIGH thanks to Thee we owe, O Christ!
    For Thy dear servants of the pen—
Apostle and Evangelist—
    Whereby Thou art made known to men.

They tell us all Thou saidst and didst;
    And all Thy glorious goodness show;
Make Thee a presence in our midst,
    Acting and speaking here below.

We sit beside Thee at the sea;
　　We're made companions of Thy walk;
Our hearts within us burn, while we
　　In silence listen to Thy talk.

We learn the lesson of Thy looks,
　　And are encouraged to draw near;
More than the lore of all the books,
　　Thy welcome whispered in our ear.

When Thy sweet lips forgiveness speak,
　　And we can claim Thee as our Friend,
Naught more in heaven or earth we seek,
　　Our wants and wishes have an end.

THE SON OF THE LAW.

IT is true in one sense, though not in another, the Life given in the Four Gospels is incomplete. Of the events of Christ's Infancy and Childhood to the age of twelve, and of the intervening years up to thirty, all record is wanting. As it was left it remains. Like some matchless *torso* of divine art, it defies addition or supplement. We should not know how divine was the divine were it not for the human. The Apocryphal Gospels, so called, are ancient attempts to piece out the record and fill up gaps. The difference is infinite. Infidelity admits it. Renan says: "They can in no wise be put on the same footing as the Canonical Gospels; they are flat and puerile amplifications based on these, and without value." Instead of a God we have a vulgar magician. Portent is piled upon portent, marvel upon marvel, and that without end. Miracle is made cheap; and omnipotence is brought into contempt by the frequency and triviality of the occasions upon which it is exercised. Divorced from use, made a child's puppet and plaything, employed as an instrument of boyish sport or boyish mischief, what profanation to call this the power of God!

We are naturally shocked. But, it may be, no profanation was intended. The low ideal was in fault. The stream cannot rise higher than its source. What is not in the mind cannot come out of it. As is the worker so is his work. The masterpiece is not simply the outcome of the master, but is the master. The art is the artist. Apollo Belvedere, for example, is mind in marble. It is the superlative of him who created it. It was more than mere cunningness of hand that produced for the admiration of after ages such matchless symmetry, power and grace. The hand might copy but it could not create. The god has shot his arrow, and he is calmly watching its flight. There is the assurance and ease of superior power—power that costs no effort and is never exhausted. Men call it a magnificent conception, and so it is. In sculpture it is first, and there is no second. Still its scope is narrow. It expresses but one thought. It is limited to hinting a single act. It is the god of a moment. But the representing of that one moment worthily has sufficed to make the author immortal.

The sun-god of the Greeks is not the Sun of Righteousness. In an artistic sense, Jesus is more than Apollo. He is an infinitely higher conception — grander, more complex, more difficult. Here the ideal presentment respects not a single attribute or act, but a character; not a moment, but a life. The magnitude of the task it is impossible to exaggerate. No epic elevation that was ever reached approaches "the height of this great argument." Melodious Homer sang:

> "Achilles' wrath to Greece the direful spring
> Of woes unnumbered."

His hero was of the vulgar type, swift of foot and large of limb. But in this case it is no earthly hero, but the unique, the unimagined; a being descended from another sphere, having no equal and no fellow: standing on the apex of two natures—the glory and perfection of both; a radiant presence in a dark world, divine in every word and act, swift to pity and powerful to save. To increase the marvel, we have four artists instead of one, each working apart; on the mythical hypothesis, idealizing and fabling apart; giving to "airy nothing a local habitation and a name:" or, on the contrary supposition, that Christ was a real person, catching and embodying the ethereal essence of a divine life spent on the earth; fixing the floating image; and presenting, not in vague outline, but in complete living portraiture of form and feature, expression and color, an exact copy of an unparalleled original. As the artists are four, so there are four distinct portraits, which by some miraculous chance are seen to be but different aspects of the same divine face, and no other; and all so powerfully drawn, as to make Apollos seem cheap and Iliads poor. How came it to pass? Was it original genius or divine inspiration that raised the humble authors of the Gospels so high above a Phidias, a Homer, or a Plato? Each of these has been called divine, but none of their works is stamped with a visible signature of divinity, like those of Matthew, Mark, Luke and John.

Now should any one ask, How do we know that the Gospels are not "cunningly devised fables," and Christ is not an invention of men? the answer is ready. Because, as Rousseau said long ago, "It is not thus that men invent;" and, as the author of "Ecce Homo" in like manner argues, "The Christ of the Gospels is not mythical, for the character these portray is so peculiar as to be altogether beyond the reach of invention both by individual genius, and still more by what is called 'the consciousness of the age.'" On the supposition there was no such person, both agree in saying the Gospels were impossible. The last writer speaks of "temperance in the use of supernatural power as the masterpiece of Christ—a moral miracle." And truly we know of nothing which more strikingly distinguishes the Christ of the New Testament from the Christ of fable than this restraining of His almightiness; making its puttings forth, so to speak, comparatively rare and reluctant; never wielding it for display, and never for His own benefit. When had it ever entered into the heart of man to conceive of One thus clothed with an idle omnipotence — possessing all power, but in the spirit of a divine self-abnegation refusing to use it in the direst extremities; and, when hanging in helpless agony upon the cross, meekly unmindful of the taunt, "He saved others; Himself He cannot save?" Rousseau is right in saying that it is not thus men invent. No human imagination could ever reach the miraculous fineness of such an ideal. All of the four Gospels are full of divinely delicate touches which declare their inspiration. It is a proof unimpaired by time. Indeed it is not too much to say that we of this age are better qualified to feel the force of such evidence than were the first ages. The diamond is self-evincing. The question of when and where it was crystallized, who set or polished it, affects not its genuineness. So the Gospels. They shine by their own light, each with its proper lustre. They differ as one star differs from another star in glory. We know they are divine, whoever were the writers. That the divine light should suffer refraction in passing through human media was inevitable, but that does not change the element; and this satisfactorily accounts for all variations. The

Evangelists, as somebody remarks, "were not God's pens but God's penmen."

Everything the canonical Gospels are, the apocryphal Gospels are not. They are the antitheses of each other. It is not resemblance but contrast. They represent the extremes of divine wisdom and human silliness. We need no Peter to tell us that Simon Magus, who offered money to buy the Holy Ghost, was a vulgar impostor; and no Paul to inform us that it was the garrulous gossips and beldames of the chimney corner who were the concocters of those "profane and old wives' fables," which make up the substance of the apocryphal (misnamed) Gospels. The most minute and characteristic and longest of these, the Arabic *Gospel of the Childhood of Jesus*—used it is supposed by Mahomet in the compilation of the Koran—has not only the same parentage as the Arabian Nights, but the prodigies related are just such as befit the Afrite of the lamp and the bottle—incredible not because they are marvelous, but because they are monstrous. For it is admitted that strangeness is no test of truth—truth is strange, stranger than fiction. There are other marks by which "Jack the Giant Killer," the myth of the nursery, is known not to be a true story.

xii

Because there are myths, however, it does not follow there is no history. Strauss' boasted " apparatus for causing the miracles of the evangelic history to evaporate into myths," "has," to use the words of Renan, " been laid aside, and satisfied nobody ;" and a like fate awaits, if it has not already overtaken, his own "legendary hypothesis," offered as a substitute. For these men who deny Christ's miracles, cannot well deny Himself, and He is the greatest miracle of all : a mighty miracle apart from His miracles. If a creation, who created Him ? What greater God ? Or is He an effect without a cause ? Whence that influence which has moulded the nations and made Christendom ? Is it so that this miraculous Nile, whose timely overflows continue to fertilize the world, had its origin in a miraculous nothing ; or, what would be still more miraculous, in some foul puddle of imposture not yet dried up ? Whence Christianity if there was no Christ ? But admitting a Christ, we must believe either that He was more than man or a deceiver. Which was He, a charlatan or a God ? If the latter, miracles would be His most proper credentials as attesting His lordship over Nature as well as under it. They are logical and consequent. Antecedent improbabilities, upon which infidelity lays so much stress, are then all on the other side. An omnipotent cause must be equal to an omnipotent effect. To deny this is to annihilate science.

But while Christ wrought miracles, He was no mere thaumaturgist. What He did was not simply wonderful—a sorcerer's trick might be that—but God-worthy; wholly divine, not semi-diabolic. He cast out devils, not by Beelzebub but with the finger of God. Scientists, credulous about many things, are incredulous in respect to the genuineness of Christ's miracles, because they were not there to see and test them. Men in those unscientific days, they think, might very easily be the dupes of appearances. But what is it that stamps a miracle? The chief criterion is its character. A miracle immoral or foolish is a contradiction in terms. It is impossible that such an one should bear the divine image and superscription. Coming from God, it must be worthy of God. It must have function and use. It must articulate and move in harmony with the hinges and joints of a compagination, which is likewise of God. To dislocate it, to tear it from its connections, and view it apart, is as absurd as to treat the spring of a watch in that manner. A miracle is a truth as well as a fact; and scientists, if they want to test Christ's miracles, can test them now as well as then. The miracles are present if the author is not. There might be trick and they be not able to detect it; but there is no room for deception in regard to the diviner half—the character—which infallibly distinguishes between the genuine and the spurious. One might as easily confound the oracular gems on the breast-plate of Aaron with dull bits of glass or pebbles by the road-side. Christ proves His miracles, and His miracles prove Him.

To feign a miracle may seem easy, but it is not; for every true miracle requires a just setting. The occasion must be a proper one, the reason sufficient, and the worker competent and accredited. A divine intervention is only justified by a necessity—"Nec Deus intersit nisi dignus vindice nodus"—a useless miracle were an indecency and an outrage. If the kingdom of Nature is to suffer violence, it must be a holy violence, directed by divine wisdom to a divine end. To create the exigency which would make a miracle proper is beyond the reach of human invention. Certain it is, that all attempts, ancient and modern, at miracle-making no less than at God-making, have been profane and miserable failures; and it is not without good grounds that we dare to characterize all apocryphal and legendary addenda to the miracles of the New Testament, of which we have any knowledge, as alike foolish and blasphemous. Falsehood can in no case be complemental to truth—the conjunction is always monstrous.

Christ is complete and sufficient as He is. He does not stand in need of either infidel apology or infidel panegyric; and until we have better proof than we have yet had of infidel ability to make a better one, we beg leave to cling to the old. Strauss is already obsolete. Renan is obsolescent. Sneering scientists of to-day will be forgotten to-morrow. But Jesus lives forever.

JOHN THE BAPTIST.

THE Prophet of the Voice !*
Made, by Jehovah's choice,
His Messenger to go before His face !

---

* The Rev. William R. Williams, D. D., S. T. D., LL. D. (1804-1885), in his Lecture on John the Baptist, aptly designates him as Prophet of the *Voice*, in contradistinction from Prophet of the *Pen*. Dr. Williams, on his last visit to Deerhurst, brought with him, for Dr. Coles' examination, a very rare Latin book, of which he had but recently become the owner. This volume contains upon its fly-leaves notes and comments in Dr. Williams' own penmanship, as neatly and as carefully executed as if done by a master engraver.

JOHN THE BAPTIST.

   He in the desert bred,
   On hermit's diet fed,
A coat of camel's hair his loins embrace.
Hark! hark! I hear his warning cry:
"Repent! Reform your lives! the Reign of Heaven is
  nigh."

   Full loud the thunder rolls
   O'er conscience-smitten souls,
And all the land is filled with solemn fears:
   To him vast numbers press
   Out in the wilderness,
And he baptizes them, baptized before in tears;
But Pharisees and Sadducees drives hence,
Devoid of these wet proofs of honest penitence.

   None of the prophets old,
   So lofty or so bold!
No form of danger shakes his dauntless breast:
   In loneliness sublime,
   He dares confront the time,
And speak the truth, and give the world no rest:
No kingly threat can cowardize his breath,
He with majestic step goes forth to meet his death.

Truth may seem stern and proud
To the misjudging crowd;
But Christ's forerunner loving is and mild :
I hear the tender moan
Of pity in each tone—
A father grieving o'er a wayward child :
Note too, how meanly he himself doth rate,
"Myself am a low nothing, Christ alone is great."

THE BAPTISM.

AT the ripe moment, like the punctual sun
Not slow nor making haste, then Jesus—One
On whom the ages wait, for whom the spheres
Make willing circuits, after thirty years
What time was veiled His Godhead, having grown
From infancy to manhood all unknown—
Leaving His home at Nazareth, journeys on
From Galilee to Jordan unto John,
To be baptized of him.   *   *   *   *
Shrinking with felt unworthiness and shame,
John spake opposing Him: "I have no claim

To this high honor: I have need to be
Of Thee baptized, and comest Thou to me?"
  And Jesus said, "Now suffer it for thus
Complete obedience becometh us.
God sent thee to baptize, and it is fit
That I should ratify and thou submit.
That I as FULFILLER should fulfill
Each jot and tittle of God's righteous will."
  Then yielded he, for how could he withstand
The gracious urgency of that command.
  O Jordan! from thy crystal source—the crests,
The top, the springy sides, the streaming breasts
Of dewy Hermon—look! for thou hast heard
The wind-borne tidings of that whispered word.
Come down from Lebanon! make haste and come
With many a sparkling leap from thy high home!
Pure as the snows in which thou hast thy source,
Flow clear, receive no soil in all thy course!
Steep is the way and facile for thy feet;
Fly swift, for that the moments too are fleet!
The good news telling as thou sweep'st along,
Thy murmurous gladness breaking into song.
With arrowy speed through wondering Merom dart!
Let awed Gennesaret its waters part

For a straight passage! not once looking back
To see how rippling smiles pursue thy track.
Since thou must keep the channel cleft for thee
Far down below the level of the sea,
Hasten the more, and compensate delay
By swifter whirlings on thy spiral way!
Nor let the thousand links of that long chain
Thy hurrying feet entangle or detain!
Nor the rough terror of the deep descent,
Nor the mild beauty of the banks prevent
Thy due arrival at the destined place
Where John and Jesus wait a little space!
No moment lose, but time thy coming, so
That the van waters shall have passed below—
Defiled by muddy affluents let in,
And washings of the leprosy of sin.

 O happy River! conscious in each drop
From thy clear bottom to thy smiling top—
Deep calling unto deep, as rapids swift
To foaming cataracts their voice uplift
In eager proclamation, far to near
And near to far, loud shouting, God is here!
Thou, ever reverent, o'er many a steep,
With kneelings many, and prostrations deep

THE BAPTISM.

Falling and falling, low and lower fall
And kiss His feet, who is the Lord of all!
He is not here for cleansing, He is clean;
A purity like His was never seen.
He can thee wash, and, washing, holy make
The guilty, bitter, deep Asphaltic Lake.
Breast high in thee, not snow is half so white,
Nor half so spotless is the unsullied light;
Caressing eddies round and round Him whirled
In circling dance, the Wonder of the world,
He stoops to thee in all His heavenly charms:—
I see Him sinking in thy jeweled arms,
Lost one amazing moment to the sight,
Then rising radiant dripping gems of light.
And as He, praying, doth from thee ascend,
(Wonder of wonders when will wonders end)
Heaven's doors dimensionless wide open spread,
And more than Heaven descends upon His head.
The Holy Ghost, down darting from above
In volant shape and semblance of a dove,
There rests, expressing peace, and, lo! is heard
A voice from heaven that joins th' attesting word:
 "Thou art My Son, My Sole Begot, in Thee
I am well pleased. Begin Thyself to be!"

—From "The Evangel," pp. 120-141.

"JUDGE NOT!"

WE have occasion to admire the just reserve of Scripture. Its silence is sublime. What it enjoins it practices. Its language is "Judge not"—especially "Judge nothing before the time." Men are excessively prone to these judicial anachronisms—are noisily and prematurely positive; swift where they ought to be slow; forward to damn or save; to do what an archangel cannot do—unravel all the intricacies of human character and conduct, and determine the exact measure of individual guilt or innocence in a given case. We can weigh actions better than we can motives. The hand of Omniscience needs to hold the scales when hearts are to be judged. Nothing can be more foolish and indecent than the curiosity which prompts us to ask, "Are there few that be saved?" What of Jepthah? What of Solomon? We are as good as told, "That is none of your business; look out for yourself!" Certainly it is no mean proof of the superhuman origin of the Bible, that it contains no commitments of that sort.

It speaks the truth; it tells the facts, without favor or affection, with no effort to palliate or conceal. It bears faithful and true witness. It spares none—not even David, the man after God's heart. The final fates of men will be settled at the Last Judgment, and there are no impertinent forestallments of its decisions and awards. It is impossible not to see there is a divine propriety in all this.—*From "The Evangel," pp. 282–284.*

*   *   *   *   *   *   *.

WHILE no man has the right to say that the virtuous heathen, who have never heard the Gospel, will not be saved; it is still true, that the Scripture is silent upon that point. So in regard to the salvation of children dying in infancy, it is nowhere said in so many words that they will be saved, but we take it for granted that they will be. "Are there few that be saved?" is another example of that inquisitiveness which is unwilling to trust God any further than He has given His word. "Will not the Judge of all the earth do right?" Are we more righteous than He, or more loving? To insist upon answers to questions merely speculative is impertinent and unseemly.—*From "The Light of the World," p. 269.*

"THAT ALL MEN SHOULD HONOR THE SON, EVEN AS THEY HONOR THE FATHER."

(JOHN v: 19, 20, 23.)

THE bare statement is the all-sufficient proof that the consciousness of Christ's two-fold nature was never absent from Him: a single moment's divorce would have made that moment worthless to man's salvation; for it was the Divine in conscious association with the Human that gave to the obedience of the latter its unspeakable value. Assuredly that aphorism of Greek wisdom, "Know Thyself," was not unfulfilled in Him. That He did not parade and publish this knowledge is no proof that He did not possess it. That He possessed it when He was twelve years old is incidentally set forth in a way which shows that it was not something to which He had just attained, but something which He always had. It preceded His official investiture. The anointing of the Holy Ghost at His baptism had nothing to do with the fact nor the consciousness of the fact of His dual Selfhood. It seems to us a strange and preposterous notion, that the revelation of Himself to Himself needed to be delayed until His human nature should be strengthened to bear it; and that it was necessary to wait thirty years for this. No good reason can be given why a child's receptivity, and tolerance too, of any form of divine disclosure should not be equal to a man's: indeed, we know that "things hidden from the wise and prudent are revealed unto babes."

We hold firmly, that Christ's consciousness of the fact, that He was both God and Man, ran parallel with the fact itself, beginning at the beginning; that the two natures were so adjusted the one to the other as not to trench on each other's proper freedom and independence; that while they were not two wills but only one will, that will, in things human was human, and in things divine was divine. It was inevitable that there should be limitations to the human, else it would not be human, but while these limitations really existed they were, we insist, voluntary, self-imposed, capable of being set aside or transcended. That they never were transcended a hair's breadth in matters pertaining to the law of His subjection, stands to the glory of His free obedience, which being perfect, "brought in everlasting righteousness." And as this abstention involved a strenuous holding back of a present omnipotence, forming a miracle of restraint full of moral sublimity, it is easy to see how immensely the merit of that obedience was thereby enhanced. It must be a power above omnipotence that can keep it in check, and that power is duty, which is only another name for loyalty to law. This doth

> "Preserve the stars from wrong;
> And the most ancient Heavens through it are fresh and strong."

The grandeur of Christ's miracles was exceeded, if possible, by His refusal to work them. The glory of His power was excelled by His weakness. The dear hands that healed the sick and raised the dead were never more adorable than when nailed in their helplessness to the bitter cross. That long incognito, when, though conscious of His divine Sonship, He was content to pass as the son of Joseph the carpenter; that grand silent waiting and hiding of His glory, without any manifestation of impatience, through thirty unrecorded years of poverty and toil, were as truly divine, and hardly less wonderful than the loud activities of the three official years that followed, when the whole land rang with the fame of His miracles and His matchless words of grace and wisdom. We know not what unimagined glory may lie concealed in the shadow of the intolerable brightness of the inaccessible light which shrouds the Eternal, but it may well be doubted whether there is any reflection of Godhead which surpasses the splendor of that condescension which disdained not to stoop to the depths of man's degradation, to wear his form and garb, to adopt his stammering speech and learn his silly lore. Who would have thought that this "foolishness of God" should transcend all His other exhibitions, of which the grace shall form the theme for ceaseless celebration, when, "in super-eminence of beatific vision" all the redeemed "shall clasp inseparable hands with joy and bliss in overmeasure forever!"

This property of voluntariness in regard to all that pertained to His humanity which we have here attributed to Christ; the power at pleasure of emptying and disabling Himself; of subjecting Himself to the humbling restrictions, limitations, infirmities, not to say the ignorances belonging to the human condition; of winking out of sight, if it be lawful to use so strong an expression in this connection, His essential Godhead, when the necessities of the *role* of the God-man demanded that the man only should appear; or personating without mask two characters, and of living without metamorphosis two lives, at one and the same time—not that He was in anywise a two-faced Janus, but a Jesus, having only one face, with the same loving eyes, now beaming divinity, now wet with human tears—this voluntariness, we repeat, this free play of the pendulum of the will swinging between the finite and the infinite, with oscillations of such inconceivable sweep and swiftness, as to make it possible for Him to be God and to be man, to be in heaven and to be on earth, in conscious alternation, a thousand times in the thousandth part of a second, is the explanation, we conceive, of half the mystery that perplexes us. And while we can never hope to untie the insoluble knot, to clear up all ambiguities and reconcile all contradictions, something is gained when we so far grasp it as to bring it a little nearer to us, and in some sort of relation to things lying within our sphere.

The finite, while it hints, often helps to interpret the infinite; but of course, where there is, as in the present case, an absolute uniqueness—seeing there is "but *one* God, the Father, of whom are all things, and *one* Jesus Christ, by whom are all things"—comparison must inevitably fail in some points. This impossibility of likening the Creator to anything created is the chief reason, we suppose, for the divine interdict against making "any graven image or likeness," for the base material counterfeit narrowing and degrading the idea of the infinite Original usurps its place in the mind and terminates the worship; and the same consideration is fitted doubtless to restrain the representations of a too rampant and irreverent rhetoric. The necessities of language may require us to speak as if there were two when there is only one; and this constitutes the apology for the use of such terms as the Trinity, defined as "three persons in one God," but there is unquestionably an attendant peril which should put us upon our guard.

There is no reason, however, why we should stumble at multiplicity in unity, when we have so much that answers to it in ourselves. Our one life we have already seen is three lives; and we are in the familiar use of power not unlike that unspeakable voluntariness and versatility we have described. Standing in the blaze of noon, we look out on the divineness of earth and the infiniteness of heaven bathed in glorious sunlight, and, literally in the twinkling of an eye, by a simple act of the will which can be repeated many times in a minute, we are able to thrust it away and hide ourselves from it in the blackness of midnight darkness, and then restore ourselves to it—in a moment to put off this garment of light, and as quickly put it on. And there is not an hour of our lives that we do not illustrate in some way the mysterious parallelism of a double consciousness; two lines of thought running side by side, two sets of simultaneous and non-interfering volitions.

An immense amount of dialectical skill has been wasted in the discussion of the question, whether Christ, in the language of the schoolmen, "was not able to sin"—*non potest peccare*, or "able not to sin"—*potest non peccare*. Assuming that He was both God and Man, we are not obliged to balance between the two propositions, but accept both as true. As God, the impossibility would be of the first kind; as Man, of the second, for if as man there were not an abstract possibility of sinning, it is difficult to understand how there could be moral freedom, or reality in temptation. Doubtless the *libertas* was likewise a *beata necessitas boni*—"liberty" being only another name for "necessity," in the case of One "who was holy, harmless, undefiled, and separate from sinners;" and who stood alone among all the sons of Adam in being able to say, "The Prince of this world cometh and hath nothing in Me." John xiv: 30.

But if there is difference of opinion in regard to His ability to sin, there is none in regard to His ability to suffer. "He was a man of sorrows and acquainted with grief." "He bare *our* griefs and carried *our* sorrows," as well as His own. "The chastisement of our peace was upon Him, and with His stripes we are healed." It is said in immediate connection with His miracles of healing, "He bare our sicknesses." Does vicarious bearing mean potential transference? Are we to understand that their manifold malignity passed over to Him; that for every pang He relieved He suffered a pang? We read, Luke vi: 19, "And the whole multitude sought to touch Him; for there went *virtue* out of Him, and He healed them all." It was thus that a certain woman, who had an issue of blood twelve years, was healed of that plague. Was the "virtue" a part of His life? Were addition and advantage to the healed, subtraction and loss to the Healer? At the tomb of Lazarus, we are told, Jesus "groaned in the spirit and was troubled," and "Jesus wept." It surely was no common anguish that exhorted groans and tears from the patient Son of God. Was it in testimony of the inexorableness of law, refusing to restore, without equivalent, what it had taken away? In raising the dead to life, did the sorrows of death compass Him, and the pains of hell get hold of Him? If so, how it magnifies the grace! how it exalts the compassion! how it swells the debt!

Jesus had not been human if pain were not hateful to Him; and there are no pains like the pains of hunger. The impatient appetite resents delay. The hungry stomach and the hungry blood send up agonizing cries for help. If help does not come speedily, the angry organs rise in fierce revolt, and all is clamor and uproar. There is nothing wrong in all this; for these instincts are of God. Their rage is innocent. It is their duty to warn. Silence is betrayal. It is no impeachment of Christ's sinlessness that He hungered; and that the blameless organs in their blind zeal, fearing for the imperiled life, and singly intent upon quick relief from the intolerable anguish, took sides for the time with the Tempter, and maintained ceaseless wrestle with the sternness of the denial of the higher life. The desire for bread was guiltless, and under other circumstances its gratification had been lawful, nay, a duty. But not then. Why?

Jesus saw why. It is true, the reason was not coarsely evident. It may have required fineness of vision to perceive it. But His eye was single and His body full of light. Weighing all acts in scales of infinite delicacy, an inclination of the beam so faint as to defy arithmetic to express it, was instantly discerned and sufficed for conduct. Not a spot must stain His absolute whiteness. So high was the requirement, that even the imperceptible tremble of the jarred earth, caused by the tread of a passing foot, must not be allowed to disturb the perfect poise of His human innocence. We know that two lines, separated here by the diameter of the earth's orbit, long before they reach the nearest of the fixed stars, blend and become as one; and so, a deviation from rectitude so slight that to the blurred vision of sinful eyes there may seem to be none at all, would, running through eternity, become an infinite divergence.

Nothing can be more vulgar than to suppose that the power of temptation is in proportion to bigness—that to make a big temptation there must be a big object. To natures cold, calculating and already depraved, and that merely count the cost of the risks to be run, this may be so; but to the pure, and even to men of moderate virtue, it is just the reverse. The danger is in minuteness. What trips the good man is the trivial and unseen. It is the pebble that lies buried in the foot-path, over which he stumbles and falls, not great rocks and precipices. The snare is laid for him in the ground and the trap is covered. "The snare of the Devil" is concealed, otherwise it were no snare. "Surely in vain the net is spread in the sight of any bird." The infection of which men sicken and die is borne on "heaven's sweetest air." * * *

Satan always adapts his temptation. He knows his man, his strength and his weakness; his times and his seasons; all the avenues of approach—*viri molles aditus et tempora*—and fails not to take advantage of any momentary softness of the yielding heart. He throws open doors of opportunity. If there is a spark he fans it. If there is a desire he feeds it. If there is a bias he fools the bent. He triumphs in a slip as much as in a fall. * * *

EPITHALAMIUM.

WE in life's journey blindly run,
    We brave the dark of what 's to be;
    But cannot tell, what we shall see
Or suffer by to-morrow's sun.

Lifting our eyes, we catch a glance
    Of some fair face unseen before,
    It may be through an open door
Which straight is shut. We call it chance.

But yet that casual look, so brief,
    May be decisive of our fate:
    The soul, discerning there its mate,
Claims fellowship of joy and grief.

Soon marriage bells swing to and fro,
    And, with alternate stroke, repeat
    Mine, thine, in iteration sweet,
To make of twain one life below.

EPITHALAMIUM.

Hail! happy pair! by welding flame
   Of love made one, a dual soul,
   A richer self, a dearer whole,
In spirit one, and one in name.

No knife so keen as can divide
   Your new-born selfhood, or restore
   Each soul to what it was, before
You were a bridegroom and a bride.

But keener than the tempered blade
   Are thoughtless words; they cut and pierce,
   And waken agonies more fierce
Than wounds by mortal weapons made.

Beware of these! abhor as hell,
   All strife and schism, making two,
   Cutting your vital oneness through!
Divided halves could live as well.

Pursue content in pleasant ways!
   And suck the nectar of the hours,
   As bees extract the sweets of flowers,
And hive the honey of the days!

And would you not Heaven's blessing lose,
   Let prayer each morning duly rise,
   Like exhalations toward the skies
To fall at night in friendly dews!

Bend meekly to affliction's rod!
   Be sure the strokes are kindly meant!
   Together climb the steep ascent
And hand in hand mount up to God!

THE MARRIAGE IN CANA.

ON the third day, arrived in Galilee,
   Jesus refused not offered courtesy
To Him and His disciples, to attend
The nuptials of a kinsman or a friend,
In Cana, Nazareth not far. How fit
That He who marriage gave should sanction it!

  *   *   *   *   *   *

Who feeds the ravens when their food is scant,
Is not indifferent to any want:
They wanting wine, and wanting means to buy,

Would Christ by miracle the want supply?
Though chiding, at the first, the bold request,
He, afterward, His willingness expressed
By sign or word.   The means, the manner hidden,
The mother bade the servants do as bidden.
There standing were six water-pots of stone,
With room for many gallons in each one;
And Jesus said to those attending Him :
"Fill up each one with water to the brim!
Draw now, and to the governor convey!"
And they astonished hastened to obey.

And when the ruler tasted it, amazed
He called the bridegroom, and the vintage praised;
Saying,
      "All use and wont thou dost reverse,
Keeping the good 'till last, and not the worse.
Whence this delicious nectar, heavenly wine?
What suns matured it; and where grew the vine?
Not grapes of Eschol hold so rich a blood,
Which cheers, but not inebriates, like food?"

Our great Exemplar sat a genial guest,
Eating and drinking even as the rest;

Unbound by vows which, proper in their place,
Did not express the freedom of the race.
Wisdom is justified. He did not say,
This thing you may not eat, and that you may;
Wine is forbidden, you shall not drink wine!
For that would prove Him other than divine;
Since, that which formed the essence of the bane,
All juices that ferment alike contain.
What profit then, to shut and bar one door,
And leave wide open twice ten thousand more?
The secret poison, wheresoever hid,
Must be sought out, provided 'tis forbid:
And man would starve and die of very thirst,
If he must analyze all nature first.

Conscience at ease on lawfulness of use,
In view of all the evils of abuse,
Asking its duty, may receive reply,
Thundered from every quarter of the sky,
If eating meat, or drinking wine offend,
Eat not forever! drink not to the end!
What though no law expressly doth ordain;
'Tis noble, God-like, Christ-like, to abstain.

Love is that law all other laws above,
And nothing 's so imperative as love:
All comprehending, like the arms of space,
In love's wide heaven no duty but finds place:
Love oversweeps the whole, and not a part—
No law so broad as is the Christian's heart.

   To legislate each duty, were to count
Drops of a stream that issue from one fount.
God gives, since all effects are in their cause,
For narrow prescripts universal laws.
Jesus drank wine and made it: that is clear:
Let all admit it freely without fear:
Wine of the cluster pressed into the cup,
The wine of nature: yielding so much up,
'T were slander, and not candor, to do more:
'T were vile to say of Him whom we adore,
He first Himself some heady liquor sips,
Then holds the poison to His neighbor's lips;
Dispensing bowls, foul outside and within,
With wrath, uncleanness, drunkenness, and sin.

   Since wine 's not one, but many—one in name,.
Many in kind; the same and not the same;

Of hurtful strength in various degree—
There's room at least for common charity.
Void of effects, and safe, He would not seek
The unapparent bane minute and weak;
But though no pharisee to strain each gnat,
What makes the feet to err, He drank not that.
Of this be sure: though learning should essay
To trip your faith, be confident alway,
No devil leered above the wine-cup's brim;
No mocker mocked from depths reflecting Him.
He would not, never did, and could not do,
What were unworthy sinful me and you—
To men that had well drunk, present and press
Enticements and temptations to excess.
Did other proof in contradiction fail,
His character, unaided, should avail
To give assurance, stablish and define,
The wine He made was unfermented wine.
Tell if you can, unless it had been such,
Why it was requisite to make so much?
Abundance argues innocence, since He
Would not supply the means of revelry,
Just when the thirst was kindled; slope the way,
And snare their feet He taught to watch and pray.

Distrust appearances! Be sure they lie
If they eternal verities deny.
Christ's character is sure. Be not beguiled!
He who is holy, harmless, undefiled,
Could do no wrong, nor yet what tends to wrong;
Is mindful of the weak and of the strong;
Leads none into temptation. Never fear
But what the cause of temperance is dear
To Him, who needs not any should Him tell,
What is the shortest, surest road to hell.
Prove that a thing is hurtful on the whole,
Is dangerous to the body and the soul,
And you may swear that thing is not for you;
That Christ condemns it, and forbids it too.

Wine is a mocker, therefore drink not wine!
It is a Christ-like reason and divine.
All Christ's commands invariably rest
On what is reasonable and right and best.
The best is still commanded: find that out
And you may follow it without a doubt.
If it be best to drink, if safe and wise,
Then, drink! ye have permission of the Skies.
But if it be, as all experience shows,

Not best, not safe, not wise, since countless woes
Proceed therefrom in a perpetual stream,
Drink not ! it is forbid by the Supreme.

If there is wine which tends to no excess,
Then prohibition would be meaningless ;
And such there is. Learned Rabbis say, the Jews,
At marriage festivals, did never use
Fermented * wine. Of leaven, every shred
They from the Feast of the Unleavened Bread
Cast out. And at the Supper of the Lord,

---

*One thing is certain, Christ did not make *fermented* wine, not even if He made *alcoholic* wine, for there was no time for fermentation. The alcohol, if present, must have been there by a direct creation, in which case it may be safely questioned, whether in any true sense it was wine at all—that is, grape wine—any more than those factitious compounds, by courtesy called wine, but which are not wine, where the laboratory is the vineyard. There are those, who under the mistaken idea that wine to be genuine must be the alcoholic article, contend for the genuine, and yet have no difficulty in using infamous shams, which do not contain, and never did, a single drop of grape juice.

Thus far we have limited ourselves to asserting that Christ did not make intoxicating wine; whether He ever *drank* it, is another question. Here, too, His character is everything—far more than doubtful philology. Anything He drank must, we know, have been a safe and unhurtful beverage, wherein there was no "excess." For it were, as we have said, a crime to attribute to Christ conduct which necessitates defense or apology. We are not permitted to suppose that the Saviour from sin was an example of sin; that He who taught self-denial, practiced self-indulgence. Rather must we believe, that every meal He ate was a lesson of temperance, that in no case did He go beyond the satisfaction of absolute needs. * * * *

Although no wine of any kind entered into the Paschal Supper originally, and

Fruit of the vine expressly crowned the board.
As on these two occasions, chief and prime,
According to the custom of the time,
Christ only drank the unfermented juice
Of the pressed grape, we know no other use.

Thou who, blest Alchemist, canst bind and loose
The elements; and under Thee reduce
All parts and powers and properties of things;
Whose word is swifter than the swiftest wings,
Piercing the depths, where all the forces lurk
Of secret nature, powerfully to work

was added afterward, it would manifestly have been a making void and stultification of the whole ordinance to have joined to unfermented bread fermented wine.

In one point of view, at least, the appetite for alcoholic stimulants is of the nature of a physical depravity, rather than moral. It is not so much a mental bias to evil, as a perversion of vital sensibilities—a disease superinduced by the violation of physiological laws. Argument and motive are, therefore, of little avail. * * * The first step in an attempted reformation, therefore, must be the removal of the appetite, and nothing will do this but an entire abstinence from its provocatives and inducing causes. * * * The fact that alcohol serves no useful purpose in the animal economy takes away all excuse from those who drink. They drink without need. It is uncalled-for hazard and gratuitous harm.

In England, not long ago, upward of two thousand physicians and surgeons, including such men as Sir Benjamin Brodie, Sir James Clarke, Dr. Ferguson, Dr. Forbes, Dr. Marshall Hall, Aston Key, Dr. Latham, Dr. Andrew Combe, etc., united in declaring, "That in their opinion, the most perfect health is compatible with total abstinence from all intoxicating beverages, whether in the form of ardent spirits, or as wine, beer, ale, porter, cider, etc.;" and "that total and universal abstinence from alcoholic drinks of all sorts would greatly contribute to the health, the prosperity, the morality and happiness of the human race."

xiv

Miraculous transformations, which are not
By ordinary processes begot,
But by immediate act of Power Divine,
Effecting change of water into wine—
Canst, yea and dost, in every time and place,
Accomplish greater miracles of grace ;
Among the springs of thought and feeling move,
Changing inveterate enmity to love.

WINE AND NEW WINE.

Matt. ix. 17; Mark ii. 22; Luke v. 37.

IN practical matters the peasant is often wiser than the philosopher. Dr. Johnson, in the Preface to his Dictionary, wisely remarks: "I am not so lost in Lexicography as to forget that *words* are the daughters of earth, and that *things* are the sons of heaven." The celebrated Doctor on one occasion was found tripping in regard to the meaning of some word. When asked the cause of his stumbling, he replied, "Ignorance, Sir!"—ignorance of the thing defined.

"Things," as best befits their celestial origin, come first; "Words," afterwards. It must always have been so. First the thing, then the name. In the present case we have to do with Three Things: Grapes, Grape juice *before* fermentation, and Grape juice *after* fermentation. The second could not be without the first nor the third without the second. The two first must have existed from the beginning. They were and are as God made them, living and life-giving, nutritive and restorative, divinely characterized together as "the new wine found in the cluster," of which it is said, "Destroy it not, for a blessing is in it." The third comes last. It is found nowhere in nature.* It is man-made, and stands a malignant metamorphosis of the second. Its invention is attributed to Bacchus in his early youth, who, according to the apt allegory given by Bacon, "rode in a chariot drawn by tigers, around which danced deformed demons —the Muses in his train." Unlike the other two, it is a thing of evil. It is not a food, but a poison. Instead of being a blessing to mankind, it is, and always has been, a curse. What is true of it now, was true of it three thousand years ago. The laws of nature do not change.

* Alcohol is the result of decomposition, or fermentation, which is another name for decomposition.

While it does not much matter whether unfermented grape juice or fermented grape juice was first called Wine, it would really seem most natural that what was first in the order of time and nearest the parent vine, should take precedence. If Wine was not its original name, it devolves upon those who deny it to tell us what it was called prior to the Bacchanalian epoch. It were absurd to suppose that a thing of which the world was full existed without a name. If the name, wine, was extended afterwards to the artificial product and this has been allowed down to our own time to usurp the rightful honor of the vinous original, it were easy to find a parallel. Lucifer, fallen and accursed, still retains the name by which he was known in heaven.

Must, as defined in all the dictionaries, is "new wine." Beyond all question *oinos neos* in Greek, answers to *vinum mustum* in Latin, and *new wine* in English, and all refer to the unfermented juice of the grape. In Luther's translation, wherever *oinos neos* occurs in the New Testament, it is invariably rendered *must*. *Must* is from the Latin *mustus*, new, fresh, with *vinum* understood, and the Imperial Dictionary defines it to be " new wine, *wine* pressed from the grape, but not fermented." In similar terms it is defined in all the languages of Europe. To say that new wine is not wine is as absurd as to say that a new bottle is not a bottle. A thing is known by what it is called. It is mere trifling to say that what has the perpetual sanction of the highest literary and scientific authorities is unwarranted and incorrect. It is true that it is not wine in the sense of fermented wine, but it is called wine nevertheless ; and my purpose is to produce undoubted examples from the New Testament of *oinos* being used in the place and in the sense of *oinos neos, i. e.*, *must*.*

In Matt. ix, 17, we read : "Neither do men put new wine (*oinon neon*) into *old* bottles, else the bottles ("old" omitted) break, and the wine (*oinos*, alone, with *neos* omitted) runneth out." In the parallel passage in Mark ii, 22, there are the same omissions in the second clause of the verse. In Luke, it is "new wine" in both

---

* The late Rev. A. A. Hodge, D. D., one of the editors of the "Presbyterian Review," from his critical outlook, after a careful survey of the whole field, declares that *all points in dispute have their final answer* in the settlement of the one question: "Does 'Wine' standing alone, mean, as is claimed, *only and always* the juice of the grape *fermented*, and *never* the juice of the grape *unfermented;* and was the same made and drunk by Christ and used by Him as one of the elements of the Last Supper?" The case is carefully made up and fairly put. The pivot evidently on which everything turns are the words "*only and always*" so that if it can be shown in *a single instance* that the word "wine" uncoupled with "new" is clearly used anywhere in the Bible in the sense of "New Wine" or *Must*, the learning which denies it goes for nothing, and the whole argument based on that erroneous assumption falls to the ground.

places, thus confirming the identity of the two. If *oinos neos* here means, as is admitted it does, *must*, then *oinos* inevitably means *must* likewise, seeing the two indisputably refer to one and the same thing. When *neos* (new) was no longer needed for definition it was dropped, and only the general or generic term, "Wine," was retained. It was in obedience to the same law of language that the defining adjectives "old" and "new," applied to bottles, were dropped after they had served their purpose. One only needs to omit the specific and defining words to see how pointless and meaningless all then becomes: Neither do men put wine into bottles; else the bottles break, and the wine runneth out. But they put wine into bottles and both are preserved.

What now is wanting to the completeness and absoluteness of the proof? Here we have the Holy Ghost for a witness, and a divine example of *usus loquendi*, clearly showing that *oinos* is properly used to denote the unfermented grape juice *without* the qualifying epithet *neos* as well as *with* it. The proof is certain, contemporaneous, positive, inspired and infallible; not to be gainsaid or questioned, repeated by two Evangelists, and fortified by a third—proof drawn directly from the Holy Gospels themselves and Christ's own words. We might properly stop here without adding a single word. The proof adduced is of the simplest kind, needing for its full appreciation no learning beyond the ability to spell, yet so conclusive that I cannot doubt but it would be accepted as such by any Court in Christendom. I, for my own part, would not ask to have the title to my own house and grounds supported by stronger proof.

Reference has already been made to that familiar principle which governs speech in the use of generic and specific terms of which here we have an excellent example. *New* wine is expressly named, because the similitude pointed at is based on properties which are *peculiar* to *unfermented wine*. There are three necessary factors in the case: *First*, A fermentable liquor (which excludes, of course, any liquor that has undergone fermentation already); *Second*, The possible presence of a ferment liable to be found in old bottles (*i. e.*, bottles previously used), whether made of skins or glass or earthenware, for this, by exciting fermentation in a fermentable liquor, would inevitably give rise to the liberation of a large quantity of gas, which, if confined, would operate with rending and destructive violence; *Third*, The closure of the bottle, for unless closed the gas would escape as soon as generated and cause no damage. But as the whole procedure avowedly looked to the *prevention* of fermentation, and thereby the *preservation* of the liquor in its unfermented state, the strict closure of the bottle, so as to effectually exclude the atmospheric air, formed a necessary part of it. Such was the Jewish method employed for *preserving must* from one vintage to another, which differs in no essential respect from that described by Latin writers, *e. g.*, Cato, the elder, who lived two centuries before Christ, and Columella, who was contemporary.

One cannot fail to be struck how very remarkably the two methods, the Roman and the Jewish, tally. Thus another important point is established, that it was customary in the time of our Lord to permanently preserve the unfermented juice of the grape. Why preserved, unless to be drunk? It is clear, moreover, that this process was so common as to be known to everybody, otherwise Christ would not have said, virtually, " No man " is so incredibly stupid or so ignorant (seeing the veriest child ought to know better) as to put "new wine," a fermentable liquor, in immediate contact with a ferment if he wishes to preserve it. The structure of the whole similitude goes to prove that the thing entered into the daily domestic life of the people, living in a vine-growing country, and that the name of wine was constantly applied to it.

Nobody who is acquainted with the high value of grapes, and grape juice as food (grape juice being in this respect little, if at all, inferior to milk itself, which chemically it closely resembles) will wonder that pains should have been taken to preserve and store up a means of subsistence so luxurious and so cheap. At the present day, the methodical use of grapes in quantities of from three to eight or more pounds daily, with or without other nourishment, is much in vogue at the so-called grape-cure stations in Germany and Switzerland; also in the south of France, in Italy and in Austria. At these stations, the grape-cure and milk-cure go together. When the stomach will not take the grapes by eating, the freshly expressed juice may be used. The *must** may also be bottled and employed at any time of the year.

---

* The late Rev. C. H. Spurgeon, in a letter written from Mentone, January 5th, 1891, quoted in "The National Temperance Advocate," says: "At the time I wrote (1877) I thought there was no non-intoxicating wine—true fruit of the vine and blood of the grape. We have found a true natural wine, and we use it with satisfaction to all our friends. I cannot think that alcohol is the essential point in the memory of our Lord's death. We have not as a spiritual fact found it so in our church. I do feel that for the strong to respect the scruples of the weak brother to whom intoxicating wine would be a snare, is of the very essence of Christian communion."

FAREWELL: LAND OF GENNESARET.

THE wedding over—after this first sign
   And attestation of His power divine,
Convincing His disciples—He, intent
To put fresh honor on the household, went
Down to Capernaum.   *   *   *   *

  Not long they tarried.   The Passover nigh,
He, whom the paschal lamb did typify,
The true Passover erelong to be slain,
As was His yearly wont, had willed again
To go up to Jerusalem.   'Twas early Spring,
And Morning on the hill stood beckoning—
The hill of Bashan, that high hill of God—
With forward leaning, all a-tiptoe, shod
With shoes of preparation.   Rising higher
Out of the land of worshippers of fire
The worshipped sun, with shafts of flame uphurled,
And soft salutatory light, awoke the world.

Why leaped ye, ye high hills? Ye Jesus saw
Who rides upon the heavens by His name Jah,
An earlier Sun, and rising; heard that voice,
Which makes the outgoings of the morn rejoice,
In prayer and praise uplifted, while that yet
In the deep waters of Gennesaret
The mirrored stars were shining: wafted song,
Borne on the charmed and dancing waves along,
Across the Lake, and up the farther shore,
And floating high the grassy uplands o'er
Of kine and oak-producing Bashan, woke
In you strange rapture—dumb, ye spoke,
Hearing your Maker sing. But now you grieve,
For that your Lord is ready you to leave.

Sigh your farewell, send forth a piteous bleat,
Ye hillsides! and, ye bellowing vales, repeat
The sadness! Lo, the pass among your hills
A numerous caravan already fills—
The Valley of the Passengers on the east—
To-day He joins them, going to the Feast.

Mourn, Bashan! Carmel, mourn! behind Him left:
Your pastures languish, of the joy bereft

Of His dear presence, as from parching drought.
What can ye do these weary months without
Your dew and sunshine? When no more, alas,
He shall come down like rain upon the grass,
Like showers that water plenteously the earth,
Filling the garners and averting dearth.

   Look thy adieu, Gennesaret, sweet Plain,
Garden of God! look once, and look again:
Smile through thy tears, the Lord will not refuse
Thy farewell wept in morning's glittering dews.
Retreating mountains formed thee this retreat—
This miracle of nature 'neath His feet,
This bay of land, this beautiful recess,
This earthly paradise, for 't is no less—
One backward step they took thee room to make,
Then forward one, returning to the Lake.
O rich in fountains, rich in various fruit,
Rich in all shade, where every tree takes root
And flourishes that grows in any zone,
In happy strife each claiming this its own:
The tropic palm, the walnut and the oak,
The fig-tree and the olive, vines that cloak
The bareness of the rocks with hanging grace,

FAREWELL: LAND OF GENNESARET.

Pomegranates budding in a sunny place;
Flowers of every hue, the ardent bloom
Of oleanders, and the sweet perfume
Of roses, lilies springing from the grass
Whose naked glories Solomon's surpass—
O weary, weary, weary nights and days!
Where now the blush that mantled at His praise?
At His departure all your beauties pale,
And sadness settles over all the vale.

   Begins your sobbing, melancholy moan,
Ye loving turtle-doves, ere He has gone:
Ye blue-birds, that the grass-blade scarcely bow
On which ye light, your wings are heavy now:
Ye crested larks, who customed are to fly
Up to heaven-gate, this morn ye nestle nigh
His passing feet, and have no heart to rise:
The turtles of the brook, with quick, soft eyes,
Plead for a parting look: storks grave and staid
Draw near for valediction unafraid:
All gentle things are full of tender pain,
And longing for His quick return again.
The waves that ripple softly to the shore
Whisper the wish, and at His feet adore;

They know their Lord, and His commands fulfill,
Are as He bids, tempestuous or still.

  Who scooped thy bed one hundred fathoms low
Deep toward the centre, then did farther go
Twice fifteen fathoms nearer the earth's heart,
And there thy waters sank, and by His art,
In the divine forgotten days of old,
Did rim the oval of thy cup of gold
With lofty mountains? Who, indeed, but He,
Thy Maker here, O Galilean Sea!
He on thy willing breast this morn shall float,
Who hath no need of sail or oar or boat,
But could as firmly walk thy waters o'er,
As though upborne upon a marble floor.
Why still when all things beautiful are sad
Looks snowy Hermon glittering and glad—
That giant of the north, with forehead grand,
And sovereign eye o'erlooking all the land?
Why, but because, go where the Master will,
That eye pursues Him, and is with Him still;
Smiling and blushing at the holy sight
Its snows ashamed before His stainless white.

Be comforted, who solitary mourn!
Not long ye pine forsaken and forlorn;
The darkened East shall soon your Sun restore,
And with His presence gladden you once more.
Behold, the Great Physician, in His palm
Bearing miraculous all-healing balm,
From Transjordanic Gilead shall come,
And make His dwelling in Capernaum.

Here in this City, beautifully set
On the north border of Gennesaret,
His mother and disciples, locked in sleep,
Know not He wakes to worship, perhaps, weep.
Land of Gennesaret! to thee belongs
The Canticle of Canticles, the Song of Songs.
Behold, the Bridegroom stands without, His locks
Wet with the dews of night, and softly knocks.

Calling, I heard one sweetly say,
   And knew the voice of my Adoréd:
"Arise, my love, and come away,
   Thou of the fair and polished forehead!
For lo, the winter's past, the rain
   Is o'er and gone, the flowers are springing,

         The turtle's voice is heard again,
            And all around the birds are singing.
         Green figs put forth, the vines smell sweet:
            Arise, my love, 'tis time for waking;
         Make haste, I wait thy tardy feet,
            The shadows flee, the day is breaking."

O happy days and nights! O happy bride,
With thy Belovéd journeying by thy side!
Better than wine, He'll slake thy spirit's drouth,
With the moist kisses of His heavenly mouth:
Will draw, and thou wilt follow, day by day,
With ravished footsteps where He leads the way.
Though thou art black, with condescending grace
He calls thee fair, and stoops to thy embrace.
As is the apple-tree among the trees,
So He among the sons are more than these:
Under His shadow, thou with great delight
Shall sit, and feast thy hungry heart and sight.
Chiefest among ten thousand, wholly sweet,
And lovely downward to His beauteous feet!
He hath dove's eyes, more dewy soft than ours;
His cheeks are beds of spices and sweet flowers:

His countenance is as the setting sun
Upon the snowy peaks of Lebanon.
Yea, my Belovéd's mine, and I am His;
He feeds among the lilies, pure He is:
On the chaste pillow of His loving breast,
I'll lay my weary head and nightly rest.

PORTAS VESTRAS ÆTERNALES.

Translation.

I.

LIFT ye up the eternal portals,
  O ye high and blest immortals!
    Heavenly doors wide open swing.
Comes the Lord of Angels straightway,
Nears the everlasting gateway,
    Lift ye up, admit your King!

II.

Joyful He, all white and ruddy,
Lo, He comes from conquest bloody,
    Bright in vestments purple dyed,

Glorious in His raiment holy,
Marching in His own strength solely,
    Many thousands by His side.

III.

All alone and unattended,
Forth from Heaven His way He wended;
    But returning, many brings—
Fruit of His divine affection,
Of His death and resurrection,
    Crop of heavenly harvestings.

IV.

Joy ye in the God of Zion!
Conquered hath His foes, the Lion,
    Seed of Abraham, triumphed hath.
Ruins earth no more shall cumber,
Heaven shall be increased in number,
    Guilty souls be saved from wrath.

V.

May He reign, the Vindicator,
Christ of Men, the Liberator,
    King of Mercy, Prince of Peace,

God Most Mighty, Life-bestower,
And of Death the Overthrower,
    May His praises never cease!

THE RESURRECTION.

IT OFTEN happens, that what the Scriptures leave obscure or undefined, men in their attempts to explain darken the more. As nobody was found equal to the task of piecing out the uncompleted lines of Virgil's *Sic vos non vobis*, we distrust the competency of human wisdom to supply the deficiencies of divine authorship. This is applicable to creeds, for there is in the best and most venerated of them a human element which reflects simply the knowledge of the time. Advancing science, while it antiquates so much of these as is human, leaves the divine untouched in all its primitive freshness. The real conflict is not between the inspired text, but its interpretation. Creeds have their uses, but Christ says, "Come to Me!" In that case, we have truth at first hand. We drink at the uncorrupted source. We are put into original relation with the Great Teacher Himself. Surely we can know far better by direct tasting that sugar is sweet than by report; but it is a common fault of the learned and the unlearned alike, that they rely on the say-so of men who had no better means of knowing than themselves, if as good.

Much of our ignorance is of ourselves. Our eyes are full of dust. Prejudice blinds us. * * * Christ said to Martha, "I am the Resurrection and the Life. Whosoever believeth on Me shall never die. Believest thou this?" She did not penetrate His meaning, nor try to. She had glibly expressed her belief in the Resurrection as she understood it; but whether the saying of the Master was in accordance with that old belief she did not stop to inquire. It is wonderful how contented we are in our ignorance. Our Lord's question is addressed, no doubt, to us as much as to Martha; and we, like her, not seeing perhaps how a present Resurrection, which *seems* to be asserted, harmonizes with a Resurrection which we have been taught to believe lies in the far future, pass by the remarkable declaration as something enigmatical or too profound for us.

Believers in the Resurrection may be conveniently divided into three classes:

THE RESURRECTION.

First.—Those who hold that the selfsame body will be raised up at the last day, meaning thereby all the material particles which happen to compose it at the moment of death. According to the poet Young, however, as set forth in his poem on "The Last Day," members previously lost will be supplied:

> " Dreadful to view, see through the dusky sky
> Fragments of bodies in confusion fly,
> To distant regions journeying, there to claim
> Deserted members and complete the frame."

Second.—Those who entertain the view thus expressed in the Epitaph ascribed to Milton:

> " These Ashes, which do here remain,
> A vital tincture still retain;
> A seminal form within the deeps
> Of this little chaos sleeps; * * *
> This plant thus calcined into dust,
> In its Ashes rest it must,
> Until sweet Psyche * shall inspire

---

* Psyche (Greek) occurs over one hundred times in the New Testament. In about half the cases it is rendered *life*, and in the other half *soul;* while the adjective formed from it, *psychikos*, occurs six times, in four of which it is rendered *natural*. Pneuma, with its derivatives, occurs more than four hundred times, and is rendered uniformly *spirit*, except in those cases where Holy *Ghost* is used instead of Holy *Spirit*.

> A softening and prolific fire,
> And in her fostering arms enfold
> This heavy and this earthly mould."

THIRD.—Those who hold that, while we are justified in assuming that "a seminal form" exists, it is to be looked for, not in the ashes of the urn, nor the dust of the grave, but in the depths of the immortal spirit itself, forming an essential part of it, being, in fact, the life within the life, possessing genetic aptitudes whereby, under a divine quickening, a spiritual or pneumatical body emerges. This—constituting what is called the Resurrection from the dead—differs from Christ's Resurrection chiefly in this particular, that in His case, there was first a revivification of the natural body of flesh and blood, without its seeing corruption;* and a spiritualizing or glorification of it afterwards, before His ascension. The advocates of this view conceive that it alone suits the analogy pointed at by Paul in regard to the buried seed—the likeness being properly between the living seed and the living man, not the dead body. "Dead things," as Locke observes, "are not sown; seeds are sown, being alive." It is the living acorn that contains the oak; the dead acorn, like

---

* See "The Light of the World," p. 141.

the dead body, is empty and contains nothing. It is the psyche, the tree's life, resident in the acorn, to which it owes all its glorious possibilities. It is this which, making use of its environments, builds up this lordliest of vegetable forms. Strictly speaking, life springs only from life, never from death. The seed seems to die, but does not. It descends to ascend. It clothes itself; it puts on beauty and glory; multiplies itself an hundred-fold, and is thus made fit to minister to the necessities of man; to nourish and build up the brain—and so become ancillary to thought and love and worship.

Compared with the magnificent potentialities of the human germ, those of the seed and acorn are poor and weak. Here, too, it is the indwelling psyche, infinitely enriched however by special endowments, which, in its marvelous workings under God, crowds into the period of a few brief months the accomplishments of mighty millenniums; repeating, so to speak, the miracles of creation from the beginning; passing up, step by step, from the lowest to the highest; through numerous imitative metamorphoses, culminating in the perfected form of the child born into the world.

From earliest times until now, much use has been

made, in the way of illustration, of the conversion of the caterpillar into the butterfly, but the mighty transformations which have already taken place at the time of birth leaves this poor example a thousand leagues behind. But change and ascent do not stop at birth. The infant ripens into a Newton. When man is at his best and highest, death comes. Believers of this third class regard it as incredible that, at this supreme point, there should be any pause or backward step in the march of development. They hold that death, rightly viewed, so far from being catastrophic and final, is grandly climacteric; is not a plunge downwards, but a step upwards; a mystic transition and birth into a higher life; that it is not more in accordance with Christian hope than it is with reason, that new forces should now come into play and a new body be formed to take the place of the old one; that, at once, without any yawning interval, under a divine and gracious quickening, this corruptible should put on incorruption, and this mortal should put on immortality, and that death should be swallowed up of life.

All this is exactly in accordance with the assurance of Paul, who said he knew that when the earthly house of this tabernacle was dissolved he had a building of God, a house not made with hands, eternal in the heavens; justifying his exultant expectation that, admitted to the vision of Jesus in His glorified body and seeing Him as He is, he should be like Him; that having borne the image of the earthy, he should bear henceforth the image of the heavenly; and be prepared to praise Him, from the first, for a finished and complete redemption, including that of his body —having attained to the resurrection from the dead which had been the object of so much struggle and endeavor during his natural life on the earth. As the apostle points out, that is not first which is spiritual (pneumatical), but that which is natural (psychical); afterwards that which is spiritual (pneumatical). As the psyche begets and raises up the psychical or natural body, by a like formative energy, it is thought, the pneuma (spirit) begets and raises up the pneumatical or spiritual body, resemblant but different.

In further confirmation of this view, they cite the declaration of our Lord to Martha: "I am the Resurrection and the Life," made purposely, it would seem, to correct an erroneous impression which Martha entertained, in accordance with the prevalent Jewish belief, that the Resurrection was a remote event, too remote to be available for present comfort under bereavement. Prior to Christ's coming, the few brief hints of the Inspired Scriptures on the subject of the Resurrection, had been formulated by the Rabbins into a creed. As Christ came to bring life and immortality to life, it would be a disparagement of His mission to suppose that all His teachings, in regard to the what and the how and the when of the Resurrection, had been anticipated by these men, leaving Him nothing to reveal; and so, if in His utterance on this occasion there should be found something new and different from the accepted Pharisaic doctrine, it would be no more than what might be expected. Christ's teachings and the Pharisees' run, we know, counter to each other. They materialized; He spiritualized. They externalized the Kingdom of God and were looking forward to it. He spoke of it, as both coming and having come. "It cometh not," He said, "with observation, but is within you." He emphasizes the *now*. All is *now*. I am the Resurrection and Life *now:* the Judgment is *now*. The hour cometh, and *now* is, when the dead shall hear the voice of the Son of God, and they that hear shall live. He that believeth on the Son *is* not judged. He that believeth not *is* judged already. Every day, so to speak, is therefore Doomsday; but the day of death is, in a special sense, to every individual, the Last Day, and the Coming of the Lord in the clouds of heaven, and the Day of Judgment. One hundred thousand souls (spirits) are ushered into the presence of the Supreme Judge every twenty-four hours; four thousand every hour, night and day; sufficient, one might think, to warrant a continued session. Thus one day is hardly more solemn than another. All days are solemn. "Every meanest moment rests on eternity."

It is admitted, that the language employed in describing the Last Judgment and the End of the World is bold and full of material imagery; but hardly more so than that applied to the destruction of Jerusalem. All Christ's teachings are full of similitudes. He taught in parables and prophesied in symbols. The apocalypse of the future is given in inspired tableaux—scenic representations, types and adumbrations of awful realities, true in substance if not in form.

It is unfortunate that this view—not this view either but something like it—is made repugnant to many minds by its accidental association with Gnostic and other heresies. It is certainly free from some of the difficulties which attach to both the other two, and has many things to recommend it. In regard to the first, although apparently favored by the Creeds, it is safe to say that it is based on false notions of identity, and is sanctioned by neither reason nor Scripture. Dust is not identity. Had Augustine—who held that all the matter which ever entered into the organism however dispersed here, would be made complete in quantity and quality in the Resurrection, even to the hairs cut off and the paring of the nails—known as much of Physiology as every tyro now knows, he must have seen how untenable was such a view. For what are the facts of the case? It is certain that our bodies are never two hours together wholly the same. The body of to-day is not the body of yesterday. "We die daily." Let Augustine's conjecture be judged of by the light of the following extract, taken from Dalton's work on Human Physiology: "It has been ascertained by careful weighing that rather more than *seven pounds are absorbed and discharged daily* by the healthy human subject; and for a man having the average weight of 140 pounds, a quantity of material equal to the weight of the whole body is thus passed through the system in twenty days"—tantamount to more than a ton a year. Augustine died at 75. Accepting his view as correct, the size and weight of his own resurrection body would need to be enormous. Thomas Aquinas held the more moderate view, that only the particles which entered into the composition of the body at death would be raised, but we know, that a sharp sickness—aided perhaps by medicine and a copious blood-letting just before death—can reduce the weight of the body several pounds; and it would devolve on the Angelical Doctor to give some good reason why the particles that remain should be more sacred and worthy of being raised than those taken away. Tertullian absurdly enough supposed, that the teeth were purposely made "indestructible," that they might serve as the nucleus of the new body at the Resurrection. A Jewish tradition, on the other hand, assigned this honor to a part of the *os coccygis*.

It is presumed that the insuperable difficulties attendant upon this doctrine of literal identity, led to the adoption of the second view, advocated by Drew in his able treatise, viz., that there is an indestructible germ somewhere in our present body, which is to be developed in the future. This—which is, if we mistake not, the belief now most common—agrees, as we have seen, with the third view in assuming the existence of a resident germinal principle by means of which the new spiritual body or organism is to be evolved, but differs in supposing that this descends with the dead body, and lies perdue in the grave until the end of the world, when it is first quickened. If the natural body is to be succeeded by a spiritual body, it would be in accordance with all analogy that provision should have been made in the original constitution of our nature for the metamorphosis, and so it can hardly be doubted that the genetic or active cause of such transformation has a lodgment somewhere in the human economy; and the question arises in that case, which is most likely to be its seat, the dead body or the living spirit. Could we find good scriptural grounds for believing that it goes with the spirit, then we should have no difficulty in understanding how the embodiment which takes place should be immediate, and how "the just" would have no need to wait to be "made perfect."

The difficulty of harmonizing this view with various texts of Scripture may not, perhaps, be so great as it seems. We do not think it the least of its recommendations, that it does away with the inferential necessity of an intermediate state, with its inexplicable anomalies, contradictions and twilight underground associations — its Paradise being, as many conceive it, little better than a weird betweenity, a kind of half prison, a place of exile and long waiting. What the state of the soul (spirit) is without the body, Isaac Taylor, in his Physical Theory of Another Life, tries to imagine and tell us; and, we confess, the conclusions which he reaches are by no means exhilarating. He argues, that as mind is dependent upon corporeity, its powers for the time are in a state of suspension. The intermediate period, being the chrysalis period of the soul, is, he infers, marked by the destitution of all the instruments of active life, corporeal and mental. This state of inaction is probably, he thinks, also a state of subterranean seclusion, involving perhaps an unconsciousness of the passage of time.

This picture, it must be conceded, is a far less cheering one than that given in the Westminster Confession, which distinctly affirms that "the souls of the righteous, immediately after death, being made perfect in holiness, are received into the *highest* heaven," etc. Now, as nothing can be higher than the "highest," there is clearly no room left for anything "intermediate;" but not content with this implied denial of an intermediate state, the Confession goes on to say expressly, "Besides these two places [*i. e.*, heaven and hell] the Scripture acknowledgeth none." It is silent as to the disembodied soul's mode of existence, but seems to take it for granted, that it has organs perfectly adapted to its exalted condition. Paul speaks of being absent from the body, but present with the Lord, which might be thought to imply that he believed in the possibility of the existence of the soul (spirit) apart from the body; but on the other hand, one would be led to think, from the importance which he attached everywhere to the Resurrection, that he regarded corporeity—spiritual corporeity—in a sense necessary.

Profoundly impressed with the greatness of the mystery which shrouds the subject, the writer feels that no attitude towards it becomes him but one of reverent inquiry. Therefore, he desires it to be understood, that the view set forth is propounded rather than asserted. He thinks it echoes the hope if not the belief of multitudes. If true and justified by Scripture, it cannot be deemed otherwise than desirable that it should be divorced from the error or the folly with which it may happen to be associated. For who would not like to be Scripturally certified that death was no more than the putting off of one garment and the putting on of another? that as soon as the soul (spirit) is unclothed, it is clothed upon with the vestments of eternity? It is easy to start objections, and raise difficulties against any view. On a subject involved in so much uncertainty, the writer considers it is lawful to differ. * * *

Trichotomists are those who hold to a threefold division of the nature of man, in accordance with I Thess. v: 23, which speaks of *spirit* (pneuma), *soul* (psyche) and *body* (soma), as constituting the whole person to be preserved blameless. The dichotomous view (which, by the way, is the current one and gives a distinct coloring to all the creeds) makes man to consist of two parts, viz.: body and soul.

The pneuma, or spirit, when it is distinguished from the soul, is regarded as the highest principle in man's nature, being that which distinguishes him from the brute creation, allies him to God, and forms the true ground of his immortality. Strictly speaking, it was the pneuma, or the spiritual part of man, rather than the intellectual, that fell — that is, suffered degradation and dethronement, with spiritual darkness and death as the result.

Regeneration is, therefore, the requickening of the dead or dormant fallen pneuma (spirit); and its reinstatement as the supreme regulative faculty in man, dominating all below. Standing for the godlike, it is rich in all divine capabilities, and so it would be strange if it were destitute of the power to clothe itself, that being one of the most necessary of all powers. Being in its own nature immortal, it needs an immortal body, and will have it, because it needs it, and when it needs it. Potentially present in the germ already, it is the pushing and growing force of the indwelling pneuma (spirit) that shapes the pneumatical (spiritual) body, and makes it its own. Entombed for the moment in mortal flesh, its resurrection is imminent. Like the butterfly from its rent cocoon, the embodied psyche-pneuma (soul-spirit) will spring forth winged and wonderful, and ascend to the highest heavens. Identity always lies in the personal consciousness of the Ego. It is simply Myself, and not an affair of atoms at all.

REGENERATION.

ALMIGHTY God! how small
    The accidents of birth;
Thine equal eye looks down on all
    Who dwell upon the earth.

Who dwell upon the earth,
    The Gentile and the Jew,
All men alike, wherever found,
    Thy Spirit must renew.

Thy Spirit must renew,
    Proud boasts of blood are vain;—
The lips of Truth to all declare,
    "Ye must be born again."

"Ye must be born again,"
    There is exception none;
Enlightened eyes alone can see,
    The Kingdom of Thy Son.

The Kingdom of Thy Son
    Set up the soul within,
A heavenly rule of purity
    To make an end of sin.

To make an end of sin,
    The work of grace complete,
Inclining evermore the will
    To make obedience sweet.

To make obedience sweet
    On us Thy Spirit shed;
O Holy Ghost, requicken us
    And raise us from the dead!

And raise us from the dead—
    Baptismal grace convey,
And bless the water of the Word
    To wash our sins away.

To wash our sins away
    True penitence impart;
And make us on The Crucified
    Believe with all the heart.

REGENERATION.

Believe with all the heart
  Thou verily didst give
Thy Son to die upon the cross
  That guilty souls may live.

That guilty souls may live,
  And Christ not die in vain,
May man, once in Thy likeness made,
  Thine image bear again.

Thine image bear again,
  Original and whole,
Enstamped upon his breast and brain,
  And mirrored in his soul.

And mirrored in his soul,
  As in a lakelet lie
The pictured purity and peace
  And glory of the sky.

THE MANY MANSIONS.

THEN taking bread, and giving thanks, He brake
And gave to His disciples, saying, "Take
Eat, this My body is, that 's broke for you,
This in commemoration of Me do."
He took the cup, and blessed it to their use,
Filled with the living, uncorrupted juice*
Of the crushed cluster, "inoffensive must"—†
A thing unleavened, worthy of all trust—
And, as He gave to them the purple food,
Said: "Drink ye all of it; this is My blood
Of the New Covenant for many shed;
Remember Me in this, as in the bread.
I 'll drink no more the product of the vine,
Till in God's Kingdom I shall drink new wine." ‡

"Be ye not troubled in undue degree,
Belief in God demands belief in Me.
My Father's house has mansions manifold;

---

* To symbolize a body that "did not see corruption."

† "For drink, the grape she crushes, inoffensive must."—PARADISE LOST, v. 344.
See Gen. xl: 9–11.

‡ See "The Evangel," p. 233, note.

If 't were not so, I would you it have told.
I go for each a dwelling to prepare —
A house not made with hands, divinely fair,
A body like My own. If I you leave,
I will return, and to Myself receive.
That where I am, there ye may be also.
Ye know the whither and the way I go."

Before any one rejects this interpretation as fanciful and unauthorized, let him, if he will, consider whether it does not suit the context ; and whether it does not harmonize with other Scripture. The objection that the "many mansions" are spoken of as *already* existing, would apply equally to Paul's affirmation, "We *have* a house (referring clearly, it would seem from the connection, to the spiritual body) not made with hands, eternal in the heavens." Jesus speaks in the next verse : "I go to prepare a place for you," and yet, the place is elsewhere spoken of (Matt. xxv: 34) as "prepared for you from the foundation of the world." So we read of "The Lamb slain from the foundation of the world." What is fixed in the divine purpose is considered as already existing. In regard to the many mansions, there is no need that we should figure them as dwelling-places, empty and expectant, actually existing in heaven; but as potential habitations, preparing and to be prepared for an eternal residence. Admitting that the spiritual bodies of the redeemed are meant thereby, it is not difficult to understand how that His going before would have reference to His sending the Holy Ghost with His quickening, upbuilding and shaping influences, guiding and directing the pneuma (spirit) at last in the way heretofore indicated, so as to give to every sanctified personality, at or after death, His "own (spiritual) body"; whence it would come to pass that the number of mansions would correspond to the number of the saved, and each house with its inhabitant would be distinctive and peculiar—differing, it may be, as stars differ from one another in glory. The coming again, promised in the same connection, nearly all agree, refers to Christ's coming at death. The Swedenborgian figment, that by many mansions are meant stellar worlds to which souls are distributed, finds no basis in Scripture, nor, we may add, in common sense; and to minimize the meaning to the dimensions of so poor a thought, as that there is room (space) enough in heaven for all believers, is, we think, to do injustice both to the speaker and the occasion.

Christ promised His disciples, that, having gone and prepared a place for them, He would come again and receive them to Himself, that they might be with Him. Did He come? If so, when? If He came to them at death, He came according to Philippians iii: 21—clothed with omnipotence to fashion them a body like unto His own glorious body. Manifestly it were not a full salvation, "without the redemption of the body." "The house we live in" below, is the body of flesh, wonderful beyond everything we know. And we can conceive of no "mansion" that our ascended Lord could prepare for us, even in heaven, so desirable as an immortal body suited to the needs of the immortal spirit. We feel quite sure that there is no substitute for it in the whole universe.

Another thought. The Lord's Supper, just instituted, symbolizes divine assimilation. By a believing apprehension and appropriation of Christ we are changed into the same image. He is our aliment. Our springs of life are in Him. Through Him "The inner man is renewed day by day." May we not assume that there is some reference here to the spiritual body, which is essential to the completeness of our personality as the sons of God?

EUCHARISTIC HYMN.

NOW FIRST PUBLISHED.

DEAR Lamb of God, our Food!
    We round Thy board are met,
Rememb'ring at what cost of blood
    Thyself didst pay our debt.

We see Thee stagger up
    The Mount of penal Pain,
And for our sins the dreadful cup
    Of expiation drain.

Both Human and Divine—
    The slain for us we see,
We eat the bread and drink the wine
    In memory of Thee.

Thy body we discern,
    By faith on Thee we feed;
Thyself made flesh is meat, we learn,
    Thy blood is drink indeed.

> Eternal thanks we owe;
>   Our lips shall ne'er be dumb;
> While these memorials forth shall show
>   Thy death till Thou shalt come.

HARK! CHERUB VOICES SAY.

HARK! Cherub voices say,
  "Lift up your heads, ye gates! lift up, swing wide,
Ye everlasting doors! that, side by side
    With Heaven's great Monarch, they
Whom He has ransomed, now may enter in —
His blood-bought purchase, purified from sin."

  They see Him as He is,
Incomparable in beauty. O how strange!
From glory unto glory they shall change
    Henceforth, until, like His,
Shall be the fashion of each form and feature—
The great Creator mirrored in the creature.

HARK! CHERUB VOICES SAY.

  Adore! adore! adore!
They swiftly rise, upborne on mighty pinions,
Through the immensity of God's dominions,
  They touch, they tread Heaven's floor;
With hallelujahs, psalms, and hymns of laud,
They prostrate fall before the Throne of God.

  From lips that ever burn,
Ascends glad praise from the angelic choir;
But there are sounds struck from the Saint's soft lyre,
  Which none but they can learn —
The sweet, strange pathos of whose warbled hymn
Doth ravish more than song of Seraphim.

  Unending is this bliss
The pillared firmament and all the spheres
May sink, perchance, in the long lapse of years,
  Swallowed in Night's abyss —
But to the dwellers in Eternity,
A thousand years shall as a moment be.

DIES IRÆ.

17TH VERSION—NOW FIRST PUBLISHED.

Day of wrath, that day of doom,
    All to ashes shall consume,
Whereof David witness bears,
As the Sibyl, too, declares.

O how great the trembling, when
Shall draw near the Judge of men,
To make inquisition strict,
And the guilty to convict.

Loud the wakening Trumpet's roar
Through the tombs of earth shall pour,
Gathering to that Throne of dread
All the living and the dead.

Death and Nature's' self shall quake
When they see the creature wake
From the dust, again to live,
Answer for his deeds to give.

Brought shall be the written scroll
Wherein is contained the whole,
And, on this authentic base,
Shall be judged the human race.

When the Judge shall sit, whate'er
Hidden is shall then appear;
Everything shall be made plain,
Nothing unavenged remain.

What, alas, shall I then say?
To what powerful patron pray?
How shall I the test endure
When the just is not secure?

King of dreadful majesty,
Let me shelter find in Thee;
Thou who dost most freely save,
Fount of good, I mercy crave.

O remember how my guilt
Was the cause Thy blood was spilt!
Mind the sorrows of Thy way,
Lest I perish on that Day!

Me Thou sought'st with toil and loss,
Didst redeem me on the Cross
By Thine agony and pain,
Let such labor not be vain!

Righteous Judge of Vengeance, who
Art, though just, forgiving too,
Cancel Thou my debt immense
Ere that day of recompense.

Like a culprit, guilt and shame
Cheek and brow and neck inflame;
Me a groaning suppliant spare,
Bowed in agony of prayer.

Thou who Mary's heart didst cheer,
And the robber's prayer didst hear,
Hast refused not to bestow
Humble hope on me, also.

Though my prayers unworthy be,
Great is Thy benignity;
Grant that succor I require,
Lest I burn in endless fire.

When, disposed on either side,
Sheep from goats Thou shalt divide,
Far from these, O let me stand
With Thy flock at Thy right hand.

While the damned away are driven,
And to sharpest flames are given,
Call me from Thy throne on high,
With the blessed to draw nigh.

DIES IRÆ.

THE 18TH VERSION, NOW FIRST PUBLISHED, WITH ADDITIONAL RENDERINGS OF THE 1ST, 5TH, 6TH, 7TH, 8TH, 11TH, 13TH AND 14TH STANZAS.

1 DAY of wrath, that day amazing,
   High the bannered Cross upraising,*
   While the universe is blazing!†

* Crucis expandens vexilla. The reading of the Parisian Missal.

† 1—*a* Day of wrath, that day of trouble
When the world shall burn as stubble,
Of which there is witness double.

b Day of wrath! O day amazing!
Prophets down the ages gazing
See the whole creation blazing.

DIES IRÆ.

2 O what terror! O what quaking!
As the Judge His way is taking,
Inquest strict in all things making.

3 Hark! the Trump's reverberations,
Through the graveyards of the nations,
Scattering divine citations!

4 Death and Nature stand confounded,
As the buried dead astounded
Rise to answer summons sounded.

5 Mystic Book of God's own penning,
Awful Record of men's sinning,
Shall be read from the beginning. *

---

* 5—a   Mystic Book of God's own penning,
Record of each act of sinning,
Shall be read from the beginning.

b   Mystic Volume of God's penning,
Perfect record of men's sinning,
Shall be read from the beginning.

c   Book, true record of man's sinning,
While the thread of life was spinning,
Shall be read from the beginning.

d   Written Book of registration
Of men's deeds from the creation
Shall be brought for attestation.

DIES IRÆ.

6 When the Judge enthroned shall hover,
All that's hidden He'll uncover,
Unavenged naught be passed over.*

7 Guilty fears my heart assailing—
Ah! what plea will be availing,
When the just man's cheek is paling! †

8 Mighty King and formidable!
Free Thy grace and admirable,
Save Thou me, Thou who art able! ‡

* 6   When the Judge shall sit, all hidden
Guilt shall spring to light unbidden,
Right no more be overridden.

† 7—a   Guilty fears my heart assailing—
Then what help will be availing,
When the just man's cheek is paling!

     b   Ah! what prayer shall I then utter,
To what Patron my fears utter,
When the hearts of just men flutter.

‡ 8—a   Mighty King and formidable!
Free Thy grace, Thy promise stable,
Save Thou me, Thou who art able.

     b   Dreadful King, Thy word fulfilling,
Grace most free on men distilling,
Me to save be not unwilling.

     c   Mighty King and formidable!
Free Thy grace unmeritable,
Save Thou me, Thou who art able!

     d   King of Kings! dread Power of powers!
High o'er all Thy free grace towers,
Deign me drop of heavenly showers!

     e   King with dread all Nature filling,
Grace most free on men distilling,
Me to save be not unwilling.

9   Jesus kind, do not refuse me!
    O remember Thou didst choose me,
    Lest Thou on that Day shalt lose me!

10 Seeking me Thy tired feet bore Thee,
    Cruel nails for my sake tore Thee,
    Let all fail not, I implore Thee!

11 Righteous Judge, I make petition—
    Of my sins grant full remission,
    Ere that Day of Inquisition!*

12 Hear my groans to Thee ascending,
    Contrite sighs with blushes blending,
    Spare me, at Thy footstool bending!

* 11—a   Just Avenger, heart appalling!
         Pity me, upon Thee calling!
         Me absolve—that Day forestalling!

    b   Righteous Judge, my heart appalling!
         Pity me, O hear me calling!
         Me forgive, that day forestalling.

    c   Righteous Judge, to guilt appalling!
         Pity me, O hear me calling!
         Me forgive that day forestalling.

13 Thou who stilledst Mary's crying,
   Heard'st the Thief when he was dying,
   Hope me gavest, me applying.*

14 Not a thousandfold recital
   Of my prayer can give me title—
   Endless fire my just requital!†

15 When the goats afar are driven,
   Place be with Thy sheep me given,
   On Thy right hand, King of Heaven!

16 When the fiery pit and hollow,
   Yawning wide the wicked swallow;
   Where Thou ent'rest let me follow!

---

* 13—*a* Thou who Mary's weeping stilledst,
       And the Robber's prayer fulfilledst,
       Once with hope my bosom thrilledst.

   b Thou absolvedst Mary crying,
      Heard'st the thief when he was dying,
      Hope me gavest to Thee flying.

   c Thou who stilledst Mary's crying,
      Heardst the Thief when he was dying,
      Hope vouchsafedst me applying.

† 14   Not a thousandfold recital
       Of my prayers would be requital
       But Thy grace can give me title.

THE NEW JERUSALEM.

REVELATION, CHAPTER XXI.

[NOW FIRST PUBLISHED]

JERUSALEM of golden fame—
    When shall my longing eyes
Behold that great Metropolis
    And wonder of the skies?

I read in the Apocalypse,
    The City lies foresquare,
And has great walls exceeding high,
    And gates beyond compare.

Its walls are built of jasper smooth;
    The City of pure gold;
Its twelve foundations are adorned
    With gems of worth untold.

The first foundation jasper is;
    The second, sapphire called;
The third is chaste chalcedony;
    The fourth, the emerald;

The fifth, the yellow sardonyx;
　The sixth, the reddish sard;
The seventh, the chrysolite pale green,
　The eighth, the beryl hard;

The topaz ninth, the chrysoprase
　The tenth is in the list,
Th' eleventh is the hyacinth;
　The twelfth, the amethyst.

The twelve gates are twelve pearls, one pearl
　Each gate through which to pass;
The streets are pure and burnished gold,
　Transparent like to glass.

Therein no temple is, no need
　To worship God afar,
The Lord Almighty and the Lamb
　Themselves the temple are.

The City needs nor sun nor moon
　To shine upon it, for
God's glory and the Lamb's shall be
　Its light forevermore.

The gates therein are never shut
  By day (of night there's naught);
The glory and the honor of
  The nations are there brought.

Nothing unclean can enter, nor
  Liars, nor sons of strife,
But only those whose names appear
  In the Lamb's Book of Life.

River of Life, as crystal clear,
  From secret fountain flows—
The throne of God and of the Lamb—
  And warbles as it goes.

On either side, in the street's midst,
  The Tree of Life stands green,
That bears twelve sorts of fruits—each month
  Still new fruit there is seen.

And the Tree's leaves likewise are meant
  The nations' hurt to heal—
Such pity is there in God's heart,
  Such love for human weal.

No curse is there—His servants shall
   Him serve, each in his place;
His name shall in their foreheads be
   And they shall see His face.

Jerusalem of golden fame—
   When shall my longing eyes
Behold that great Metropolis
   And wonder of the skies?

I, John, the Holy City saw,
   Adorned with many a gem
Like to a bride, come down from God—
   The New Jerusalem—

And out of heaven I heard a voice
   Proclaim aloud and tell:
"God's tabernacle is with men,
   And He with them will dwell.

"And He shall ever with them be;
   No grief shall more arise;
His hands shall wipe away all tears
   Forever from their eyes."

THE NEW JERUSALEM.

And He that sitteth on the throne
  Said, "I make all things new;
Write! for these words I utter are
  Most faithful and most true.

"I Alpha and Omega am,
  Beginning and the End;
Water of Life to all who thirst
  I freely will extend,

"To him who overcomes shall fail
  Of all these things not one;
And I will be his Father God,
  And he shall be My son."

Then a great voice was heard in heaven,
  As of a mighty throng,
Proclaiming, "Hallelujah! power
  And rule to God belong."

Jerusalem of golden fame—
  When shall my longing eyes
Behold that great Metropolis
  And wonder of the skies?

Sit laus Patri cum Filio,
Sancto simul Paraclito,
Nobisque mittat Filius
Charisma Sancti Spiritûs.

Praise to the Father with the Son
And Comforter, dear Three in One;
And may the Son on us in love
Send down the Spirit from above.

WORKS

OF

ABRAHAM COLES, M.D., LL.D.

REVIEWED BY

EMINENT CRITICS.

WORKS OF ABRAHAM COLES, M.D., LL.D.

LATIN HYMNS, in Four Parts, viz.:
    I. DIES IRÆ, in Thirteen Original Versions. Sixth edition. (1892.)
    II. STABAT MATER (Dolorosa). Third edition.
    III. STABAT MATER (Speciosa). Second edition.
    IV. OLD GEMS IN NEW SETTINGS. Third edition.

    All bound together, with biographical and critical prefaces, with full-page illustrations of: "The Last Judgment," by Michael Angelo; "Christus Remunerator," "St. Augustine and His Mother," "Faith and Hope," by Ary Scheffer; "Mary at the Cross," by Paul Delaroche; Raphael's "Madonna di San Sisto," the gem of the Dresden gallery; "Ecstasy and Prayer," by Ch. Landelle; etc., etc. Crown, 8vo, pp. 249. $3.00.

THE MICROCOSM AND OTHER POEMS.

    Including three additional versions of the "Dies Iræ," National Lyrics, and Hymns for Children. Beautifully illustrated. Crown, 8vo, pp. 348. $2.50.

THE LIFE AND TEACHINGS OF OUR LORD.
In Verse.

    Being a complete, harmonized exposition of the four gospels, with original notes, etc. A cyclopædia of religious knowledge. Two volumes in one.
    Illustrated with Munkacsy's "Christ Before Pilate." Crown, 8vo, pp. 800. $2.50.

THE LIFE AND TEACHINGS OF OUR LORD.

In Verse. Two volumes, viz.:

Vol. I. THE EVANGEL.

> Illustrated with twenty-eight full-page "artotype' copies of: "Ecce Homo," by Guido Reni; "The Four Evangelists," by Thorwaldsen; "Salvator Mundi," by Carlo Dolce; "The First Death," by Adrian V. Werff; "The Annunciation," by Prof. E. Deger; "The Visitation," by Bida; "Golgotha," by J. L. Gerome; "La Notte," by Correggio; "The Presentation in the Temple," by W. T. C. Dobson; "The Magi Going to Bethlehem," by J. Portaels; "The Flight into Egypt," by Dorothea Lister; "The Massacre of the Innocents," by Guido; "The Shadow of the Cross," by Phil. R. Morris; "Nazareth," by W. T. C. Dobson; "The Good Shepherd," by Murillo; "The Finding of the Saviour in the Temple," by W. Holman Hunt; "The Voice in the Wilderness," by Guido Reni; "Jesus, the Christ," by Ary Scheffer; "The Scapegoat," by W. Holman Hunt; "The Temptation," by Ary Scheffer; "Christus Consolator," by Ary Scheffer; "The Holy Family," by F. Ittenbach; "Christ's Mother and Brethren," by Bida; "The Marriage at Cana," by Paul Veronese; "Christ by the Sea of Galilee," by Bida; "Jeptha's Return," by Leon Glaize; "Ruth and Naomi," by Ary Scheffer; "The Cleansing of the Temple," by Barthelemy Manfredi; "Invocation and Petition," by Ch. Landelle; etc. Crown, 8vo, pp. 405. $3.50.

Vol. II. THE LIGHT OF THE WORLD.

> Including translations of various Latin Hymns and illustrated with full-page "artotype" copies of: "Christ Before Pilate," by Munkacsy; "The Good Shepherd," by Dobson; "Christ and His Disciples on Their Way to Emmaus," by B. Plockhorst; etc. Crown, 8vo, pp. 395. $2.50.

A NEW RENDERING OF THE HEBREW PSALMS INTO ENGLISH VERSE.

> With notes, critical, historical and biographical, including an historical sketch of the French, English and Scotch metrical versions. pp. 300. $1.25.

MAN, THE MICROCOSM; AND THE COSMOS. Fourth edition. (1892.)

> With full-page "artotype" illustrations of "The Transfiguration," Raphael's last and grandest work; "Salvator Mundi," by Carlo Dolce, and the "Aurora," by Guido Reni, "the artist's finest work. Well suited for use as a text-book in Colleges and Theological Seminaries. $1.25.

MAN, THE MICROCOSM. Fifth (Physicians') edition. (1892.)

> With portrait and biographical sketch of the author, and illustrated with eight full-page illustrations, viz.: "Ambrose Paré, the Father of French Surgery;" "Edward Jenner, the Discoverer of Vaccination;" "Andreas Vesalius, author of the immortal work, 'De Corporis Humani Fabrica;'" "William Harvey Demonstrating to Charles I, His Theory of the Circulation of the Blood;" Rembrandt's famous "Lesson in Anatomy—Prof. Tulp and His Pupils;" the "Apollo Belvedere," from a photograph of the original statue; the "Venus de Medici, which from its exquisite proportions and perfection of contour has become the most celebrated standard of female form extant;" "Theodor Billroth and his Clinical Assistants, Vienna;" etc. $2.50.

An appropriate gift to a physician.

For sale by all booksellers; or sent, at our expense, to any address, on receipt of price mentioned.

D. APPLETON & CO., Publishers, New York.

CRITICS AND CRITICISMS.

CRITICS AND CRITICISMS.

Richard Grant White (1821–1885), in "The Albion":

"We commend the volume, 'Dies Iræ, in Thirteen Original Versions,' as one of great interest; and an admirable tribute from American scholarship and poetic taste to the supreme nobility of the original poem. Dr. Coles has shown a fine appreciation of the spirit and rhythmic movement of the Hymn, as well as unusual command of language and rhyme; and we much doubt whether any translation of the 'Dies Iræ,' better than the first of the thirteen, will ever be produced in English, except perhaps by himself. . . . As to the translation of the Hymn, it is perhaps the most difficult task that could be undertaken. To render 'Faust' or the 'Songs of Egmont' into fitting English numbers, would be easy in comparison."

The Rev. Samuel Irenæus Prime, D. D. (1812–1885), in the "New York Observer":

"The book is a gem both typographically and ntrinsically; beautifully printed at the 'Riverside Press,' in the loveliest antique type, on tinted paper, with liberal margins, embellished with exquisite photographs of the great masterpieces of Christian art, and withal elegantly and solidly bound in Matthew's best style, a gentlemanlike book, suggestive of Christmas and the centre-table; and its contents worthy of their dainty envelope, amply entitling it as well to a place on the shelves of the scholar. . . . The first t.. o. the thirteen versions of the 'Dies Iræ' appeared in the 'Newark Daily Advertiser' as long ago as 1847. They were extensively copied by the press, and warmly commended—particularly by the Rev. Drs. James W. Alexander and W. R. Williams, scholars whose critical acumen and literary ability are universally recognized—as being the best of the English versions in double rhyme; and examples of singular success in a difficult undertaking, in which many, and of eminent name, had been competitors. The eleven other versions are worthy companions of those which have received such eminent endorsement. Indeed, we are not sure but that the last, which is in the same measure as Crashaw's, but in our judgment far superior, will please the general taste most of all."

William Cullen Bryant (1794–1878), in the New York "Evening Post":

"There are few versions of the Hymn which will bear to be compared with these; we are surprised that they are all so well done."

James Russell Lowell (1819–1891), in "The Atlantic Monthly":

"Dr. Coles has made, we think, the most successful attempt at an English translation of the Hymn that we have ever seen. . . . . He has done so well that we hope he will try his hand on some of the other Latin Hymns. By rendering them in their own metres, and with so large a transfusion of their spirit as characterizes his present attempt, he will be doing a real service to the lovers of that kind of religious poetry in which neither the religion nor the poetry is left out. He has shown that he knows the worth of faithfulness."

"Christian (Quarterly) Review:"

"Of Dr. Coles' remarkable success as respects these particulars (namely, faithfulness and variety), no one competent to judge can doubt. . . . For all that enters into a good translation, fidelity to the sense of the original, uniform conformity to its tenses, preservation of its metrical form without awkwardly inverting, inelegantly abbreviating, or violently straining the sense of the words, and the reproduction of its vital spirit—for all these qualities Dr. Coles' first translation stands, we believe, not only unsurpassed, but unequalled in the English language."

"The Boston Transcript" says:

"The 'Dies Iræ' is by far the most interesting hymn to Protestants and poets, of all that our fathers used to sing or hear in a strange tongue 'not understanded of the people;' and so thoroughly has the translator (Dr. Coles) entered the circle of the old song's heat and strength that he has been carried through it again and again, and here are more than a dozen versions of the same Latin words, and an historical criticism in a strong, earnest and poetical style akin to that of the hymn itself."

Lady Jane Franklin, wife of Sir John Franklin, when in this country, met Dr. Coles at the residence of a mutual friend; similarity of tastes, and the interest taken by Dr. Coles in the search for her husband, ripened the acquaintanceship into that of friendship. From her letter written from New York, October 22d, 1860, we quote the following:

' Dr. Abraham Coles:

"Dear Sir—I cannot deny myself the pleasure of thanking you

once more for your most beautiful little book, 'The Dies Iræ, in Thirteen Original Versions,' which I value not only for its intrinsic merit, but as an expression of your very kind feelings towards me. Believe me, gratefully and truly yours."

William C. Prime, in the "Journal of Commerce":

"Dr. A. Coles has long been known to the literary world as specially successful in the translation of Latin Hymns. His renderings of the 'Dies Iræ' are familiar to many readers. He has now also prepared a book entitled 'Old Gems in New Settings,' an exquisite volume, in which we find the 'De Contemptu Mundi,' the 'Veni Sancte Spiritus, and other fine old favorites skillfully and gracefully translated. The grand hymn or poem of Bernard de Clugny, of which the extracts in this book are styled 'Urbs Cœlestis Syon,' is rendered in a style very nearly resembling the original, and gives the reader, who does not understand Latin, an excellent idea of the peculiar characteristics of the hymn of Bernard. Besides these, we have the 'Stabat Mater,' with a complete history of the noble hymn, and a very fine translation. The lovers of old hymns owe a special debt of gratitude to Dr. Coles for the good taste and the thorough appreciation and ability which he brings to the work of placing these glorious old songs within reach of the modern world. We could wish them to become favorites in every family, and they will so become in spite of their Latin origin."

The Rev. Philip Schaff, D. D., LL. D., in "Hours at Home":

"There are about eighty German translations of the 'Stabat Mater' and several English translations. But very few of the latter strictly preserve the original metre. The English double rhyme rarely expresses the melody and pathos of the Latin. Dr. Abraham

Coles, the well-known author of fourteen translations of 'Dies Iræ,' has probably best succeeded in a faithful rendering of the 'Mater Dolorosa.' * * * The admirable English version of the 'Mater Dolorosa,' which carefully preserves the measure of the original, is from Dr. Coles, who kindly granted us permission to use it."

"The Republican," Springfield, Mass.:

"Dr. Abraham Coles won fame, and sure fame, by the most poetic and truthful translations ever given of that great mediæval hymn, the 'Dies Iræ.'"

George Ripley (1802–1880), in the "New York Tribune":

"United with a rare command of language and facility of versification, this is the secret of the eminent success with which the translator has reproduced the solemn litany of the Middle Ages in such a variety of forms. If not all of equal excellence, it is hard to decide as to their respective merits, so admirably do they embody the tone and sentiment of the original in vigorous and impressive verse. The essays which precede and follow the Hymn, exhibit the learning and the taste of the translator in a most favorable light, and show that an antiquary and a poet have not been lost in the study of science and the practice of a laborious profession. In addition to the thirteen versions of 'Dies Iræ,' the volume contains translations of the 'Stabat Mater,' 'Urbs Cœlestis Syon,' 'Veni Creator Spiritus,' and other choice mediæval hymns which have been executed with equal unction and felicity.

"We have also a poem by the same author, entitled 'The Microcosm,' read before the Medical Society of New Jersey at its centenary anniversary. It is an ingenious attempt to present the principles of the animal economy in a philosophical poem, somewhat after the manner of Lucretius, and combining scientific analysis with religious sentiment. In ordinary hands, we should not regard this as a happy, nor a safe experiment, but the dexterity with which it has been managed by Dr. Coles, illustrates his versatile talent as well as the originality of his conceptions.

The Rev. James McCosh, D. D., LL. D., President of the College of New Jersey, in a letter to Dr. Coles:

"PRINCETON, N. J.

"I have read with the liveliest delight your translations of the 'Latin Hymns.' I wonder how you could have drawn out thirteen of the 'Dies Iræ,' all in the spirit and manner of the original, and yet so different. I thought each the best as I read it. * * * * I have read enough of 'The Microcosm' to see that it is thoroughly scientific."

Richard Stockton Field, LL. D., (1803-1870), in 1838 Attorney General of New Jersey; in 1862 United States Senator; in 1863 appointed by President Lincoln United States District Judge for the District of New Jersey; at the time of his death President of the New Jersey Historical Society:

"PRINCETON, N. J.

"DR. ABRAHAM COLES:

"MY DEAR SIR—With the original 'Dies Iræ' and 'Stabat Mater' I have long been familiar. They have always had a peculiar charm, I may say fascination, about them, and I have loved to repeat them. And now I have no hesitation in saying that they never have been, and I doubt if they ever will be, as well translated into English verse as they are in your volume.

"Knowing the difficulty of the task, seeing how others have

failed, I am indeed astonished at your success. With the strictest fidelity, your translations have all the tenderness, pathos and rhythm of the beautiful and touching originals. I speak more particularly of the first of the 'Dies Iræ' and of the 'Stabat Mater.' The two first stanzas of the latter are perfect.

"Your 'Microcosm,' too, is a noble poem. It has many strikingly beautiful passages. It evinces science and culture, and poetical talent of high order. You display great command of language, and great facility of versification. Your prose also is easy and graceful. I am glad of the opportunity afforded me of rendering this feeble tribute to their merits. Very truly yours."

The "Newark Daily Advertiser:"

"Dr. Coles has supplied a want and done a graceful work in "The Microcosm." What the flower or babbling stream is to Wordsworth, that is the stranger, more complex, and more beautiful human frame to our author. In its organs, its powers, its aspirations, and its passions, he finds ample theme for song. . . Everywhere the rhythm is flowing and easy, and no scholarly man can peruse the work without a glance of wonder at the varied erudition, classical, poetical, and learned, that crowds its pages, and overflows in footnotes. And through the whole is a devout religious tone and a purity of purpose worthy of all praise."

Edmund C. Stedman:

"Ced Dr. Coles' researches, made so lovingly and conscientiously in his special field of poetical scholarship, have given him a distinct and most enviable position among American authors. We of the younger sort learn a lesson of reverent humility from the pure enthusiasm with which he approaches and handles his noble themes. The 'tone' of all his works is perfect. He is so thoroughly in sympathy with his subjects that the lay reader instantly shares his feeling; and there is a kind of 'white light' pervading the whole—prose and verse—which at any time tranquilizes and purifies the mind."

The Rev. Robert Turnbull, D. D.:

"I have finished the reading of 'The Microcosm,' which has afforded me unmingled delight. It is really a remarkable poem, and has passages of great beauty and power. It cannot fail to secure the admiration of all capable of appreciating it. Its ease, its exquisite finish, its vivid yet delicate and powerful imagery, and above all its sublime religious interest, entitle it to a very high place in our literature."

John G. Whittier:

"Dr. Abraham Coles is a born hymn writer. No man living or dead has so rendered the *text* and the *spirit* of the old and wonderful Latin Hymns. * * * His 'All the Days' and his 'Ever With Thee' are immortal songs. It is better to have written them than the stateliest of epics. * * * The idea of 'The Microcosm' is novel and daring, but it is worked out with great skill and delicacy. * * * 'The Evangel' is a work of piety and beauty. The Proem opens with strong, vigorous yet melodious verse. I see no reason why the Divine Story may not be fitly told in poetry."

Rev. S. I. Prime, D. D., in "The New York Observer":

"'The Evangel in Verse,' is the ripest fruit of the scholarship, taste and poetic talent of one of our accomplished students of English verse, whose translations of 'Dies Iræ' and other poems have made the name of Dr. Coles familiar in the literature of our day. In the work before us he has attempted something higher and better than any former essay of his skillful pen. He has rendered the Gospel story of our Lord and Saviour into verse, with copious notes, giving the largest amount of knowledge from critical authorities to justify and explain the readings and to illuminate the sacred narrative. . . . He excludes everything fictitious, and clings to the orthodox view of the character and mission of the God-man. The illustrations are a complete pictorial anthology. Thus the poet, critic, commentator and artist has made a volume that will take its place among the rare productions of the age, as an illustration of the genius, taste, and fertile scholarship of the author."

George Ripley, in the "New York Tribune":

" The purpose of this volume, 'The Evangel,' would be usually regarded as beyond the scope of poetic composition. It aims to reproduce the scenes of the Gospel History in verse, with a strict adherence to the sacred narrative and no greater degree of imaginative coloring than would serve to present the facts in the most brilliant and impressive light. But the subject is one with which the author cherishes so profound a sympathy, as in some sense to justify the boldness of the attempt. The Oriental cast of his mind allures him to the haunts of sacred song, and produces a vital communion with the spirit of Hebrew poetry. Had he lived in the days of Isaiah or Jeremiah, he might have been one of the bards who sought inspiration 'at Siloa's brook that flowed fast by the oracle of God.' The present work is not the first fruits of his religious Muse, but he is already known to the lovers of mediæval literature by his admirable translations of the 'Dies Iræ.' . . . The volume is brought out in a style of unusual elegance, as it respects the essential requisites of paper, print and binding, while the copious illustrations will attract notice by their selection of the most celebrated works of the best masters."

The Rev. James McCosh, D. D., LL. D., upon the publication of "The Evangel:"

"College of New Jersey,
"Princeton, N. J.

"You are giving to the world further proof that we did ourselves honor in conferring upon you some years ago the honorary degree of LL. D. * * * * I spent several hours last Sabbath in reading your poem, and relished it very much."

Daniel Haines (1801–1877), in 1843 elected Governor of New Jersey, and re-elected in 1847; Judge of the Supreme Court; one of the committee on the reunion of the two branches of the Presbyterian Church:

"Hamburg, N. J.

"My Dear Sir—I can scarcely find fitting words in which to express my sincere thanks for your kind remembrance of me in the presentation of the beautiful copy of your recent work, 'The Evangel in Verse.' From the introduction, the proem and a few chapters, I judge it to be a work of rare excellence. The metrical composition is pleasant to the ear and eye, and is remarkable for its literal meaning. To me the greater charm is its clear and forcible expressions of evangelical truth and sound Christian doctrine.

"It is the most succinct and complete refutation of the doctrine of Darwin and Huxley that I have seen.

"The Christian world owes you a debt of gratitude for your labor and research, and heartfelt thanks to God for giving you the ability to produce a book so full of instruction, and affording so much gratification to the cultivated mind."

The Rev. George Dana Boardman, D. D.:

" 'The Evangel in Verse' is a feast to the eye and ear and heart.

The careful exegesis, the conscientious loyalty to the statements of the Holy Story, the sympathetic reproduction of a remote and Oriental past, the sacred insight into the meaning of the Peerless Career, the homageful yet manly, unsuperstitious reverence, the rhythm as melodious as stately, the frequent notes, opulent in learning and doctrine and devotion, the illustrations deftly culled from whatever is choice in ancient and modern art, these are some of the many excellencies which give to 'The Evangel in Verse' an immortal beauty and worth, adding it as another coronet for Him on whose brow are many diadems."

The Rev. Charles Hodge, D. D., LL. D. (1797–1878):

"I admire the skill which 'The Evangel' displays in investing with rainbow hues the simple narrations of the Gospels. All, however, who have read Dr. Coles' versions of the 'Dies Iræ' and other Latin Hymns must be prepared to receive any new productions from his pen with high expectations. In these days when even the clerical office seems in many cases insufficient to protect from the present fashionable form of scepticism, it is a great satisfaction to see a man of science and a scholar adhering so faithfully to the simple Gospel."

The Hon. Frederick Theodore Frelinghuysen:

"United States Senate Chamber,
"WASHINGTON, D. C.

"MY DEAR DOCTOR—Many thanks to you for having written 'The Evangel.' It is admirably conceived and executed. While the poem impresses the truth, it will lure many who would have remained uninformed to the valuable instruction contained in the Notes. The notes on Darwin, The Logos, Herod, and the miracle at Ajalon, are excellent. The poem brings out many scriptural truths, which are not on the surface. Let me say, it is a great thing to have written the book—to have your labor associated with salvation."

The Rev. Robert Lowell, D.D., in the "Church Monthly":

"Dr Coles is plainly a man of a very religious heart and a deeply reverential mind. . . . Moreover he has so much learning in his favorite subject, and so much critical instinct and experience, that those who can relish honest thinking, and tender and most skillful and true deductions, accept his teaching and suggestion with a ready —sometimes surprised—sympathy and confidence. Add to all this, that he has the sure taste of a poet, and the warm and loving earnestness of a true believer in the redeeming Son of God, and the catholic spirit of one who knows with mind and heart that Christianity at its beginning was Christianity, and we have the man who can write such books as earnest Christian people will welcome and be thankful for. . . . In this new book he proposes 'that "The Evangel" shall be a poetic version, and verse by verse paraphrase, so far as it goes, of the Four Gospels, anciently and properly regarded as one.' He makes an exquisite plea, in his preface, for giving leave to the glad words to rejoice at the Lord's coming in the Flesh, for which all other beings and things show their happiness. . . . . In the notes the reader will find (if he have skill for such things) a treasure-house, in which everything is worthy of its place. Where he has offered new interpretations, or set forth at large interpretations not generally received or familiar, he modestly asks only to have place given him, and gives every one free leave to differ. Everywhere there is the largest and most true-hearted charity. . . . The reader cannot open anywhere without finding in these notes, if he be not wiser or more learned than ourselves, a great deal that he never saw, or never saw so well set forth before."

Stephen Alexander, LL. D., Professor of Mechanics and Astronomy in the College of New Jersey:

"PRINCETON, N. J.

"ABRAHAM COLES, M. D., LL. D.:

"MY DEAR SIR—I have delayed the acknowledgement of the receipt of your beautiful 'Evangel' until I could make some return after the same fashion. Please accept my sincere thanks, as well as my congratulations on your great success. I am always interested in your books, and always learn something from them.

"With this I send a copy of my 'Statement and Exposition of Certain Harmonies of the Solar System,' which I hope may reach you safely. Please accept the same, with my respects and regards. I think the Notes at the end and the supplement may especially interest you."

Dr. Oliver Wendell Holmes:

"There is a kind of straightforward simplicity about the poetical paraphrases which reminds one of the homelier but still always interesting verses which John Bunyan sprinkles like drops of heavenly dew along the pages of the Pilgrim's Progress. The illustrations add much to the work, in the way of ornament, and aid to the imagination. One among them is of terrible power, as it seems to me, such as it would be hard to show the equal of in the work of any modern artist. I mean Holman Hunt's 'Scapegoat.' There is a whole theology in that picture. It haunts me with its fearful suggestiveness like a nightmare. I find 'The Evangel' an impressive and charming book. It does not provoke criticism—it is too devout, too sincere, too thoroughly conscientious in its elaboration to allow of fault-finding or fault-hunting."

William Cullen Bryant:

"I have read 'The Evangel' with pleasure and satisfaction The versification of the Lord's Prayer is both an expansion of the sense and a commentary. The thought has often occurred to me what a world of meaning is there wrapped up, and that meaning is admirably brought out."

Henry Woodhull Green, LL. D., (1802–1876), Chief Justice of the Supreme Court of New Jersey from 1846 till 1860, when he became Chancellor:

"TRENTON, N. J.
"ABRAHAM COLES, LL. D., Newark, N. J.:

"MY DEAR SIR—I have read as much of 'The Evangel' during the month since I received it as my leisure and the state of my health have permitted. Of its literary merits, I do not feel myself qualified to judge, but its perusal has given me great pleasure. I have been particularly impressed with the fidelity with which you have adhered to the sacred narrative, unmarred by the decorations of heathen mythology or papal fable. I regard that as no ordinary merit. I can well understand the strong temptation under which a man of high classic culture must, in a work of this kind, constantly labor, to turn from the stern simplicity of the sacred narrative to seek embellishment amid the flowers of classic fiction. To have resisted successfully such temptation, I regard as a very high merit; and I congratulate you on the production of a work, which, I cannot doubt, will redound to your own honor and the honor of OUR STATE. With high regard, I am, very respectfully yours."

Charles H. Spurgeon, writing from Westwood, Beulah Hill, Upper Norwood, speaks of "The Evangel" as "a grand volume," and concludes his affectionate letter with the words:

"Peace be to you, and every blessing. May Scotch Plains be a spot wherein Jesus dwells with a happy household. Yours very heartily."

The Hon. William Earl Dodge, (1805-1883), merchant and philanthropist, in a letter, written from his residence in New York City, to Dr. Coles:

"Mrs. Dodge and myself have very much enjoyed 'The Evangel,' having carefully read it. Such perfect conformity to the text and spirit of the sacred narrative, so beautifully transferred to verse, we have seldom found."

Thomas Gordon Hake, M. D., author of "Madeline, and Other Poems and Parables":

"12 Portland place,
"West Kensington, W., LONDON.

"I have read 'The Evangel,' and 'The Light of the World,' with deep interest, and with assurance that the learning and intelligence displayed in executing so difficult a work will secure it a lasting place in our joint national literature."

The "New York Observer":

"The skill of Dr. Coles as an artistic poet, his reverent, religious spirit, and the exalted flight of his muse in the regions of holy meditation are familiar to our readers. It is, therefore, superfluous for us to do more than announce a new and elegant volume from his pen—'The Microcosm and Other Poems.' It is rich in its contents. 'The Microcosm' is an essay in verse on the science of the human body; it is literally the science of physiology condensed into 1,400 lines. The many occasional poems that follow are the efflorescence of a mind sensitive to the beautiful and rejoicing in the true; finding God in everything, and delighting to trace the revelation of His love in all the works of His hand. Such a volume is not to be looked at for a moment and then laid aside. Like the great epics, it is a book for all time, and will lose none of its interest and value by the lapse of years. The publishers have given it a splendid dress, and the illustrations add greatly to the attractions of this truly elegant book."

The "New York Times":

"The flavor of the book, 'The Microcosm and Other Poems,' is more quaint, suggesting, on the religious side, George Herbert, and on the naturalistic side, the elder Darwin, who, in 'The Botanic Garden,' laid the seed of the revolution in science, accomplished by the patient genius of his grandson. Some of the hymns for children are beautiful in their simplicity and truth."

"The Critic":

"The long poem, 'The Microcosm,' which gives its name to the present collection, has many beautiful and stately passages. Among the shorter pieces following it, is to be found some of the best devotional and patriotic poetry that has been written in this country."

John Y. Foster, author and editor, in "Frank Leslie's Illustrated Newspaper":

"In this exquisite and brilliantly illustrated volume, the scholarly author has gathered up various children of his pen and grouped them in family unity. 'The Microcosm,' which forms one-fifth of the volume of 350 pages, is an attempt to present, in poetical form, a compendium of the science of the human body. In originality of conception and felicity of expression, it has not been approached by any work of our best modern poets. The other poems are all marked by the highest poetic taste, having passages of great beauty and power."

Hon. Justin McCarthy:

"20 Cheyne Garden, Chelsea, LONDON, England.

"DEAR DR. COLES—I am surprised to see, in looking through your volume, 'The Microcosm and Other Poems,' that you have been able to add three more versions to those you have already made of that wonderful Latin hymn, perhaps the greatest of all, 'Dies Iræ.' Certainly it is one of the most difficult to translate. I like your last version especially."

The "Examiner and Chronicle":

"The title-poem in this exquisitely printed and charmingly illustrated volume, 'The Microcosm and Other Poems,' has been for some time before the public, and has received generous commendation for the tact and skill evinced in handling a very unpromising theme. A poetic description, minute and thorough going of the human body was a serious undertaking; but Dr. Coles delights in what is difficult and hazardous. He had already associated his name forever with the mediæval Latin hymn, 'Dies Iræ,' by publishing no less than thirteen distinct versions of it. In the volume before us he gives us three more versions. The other poems will not detract from the author's previous reputation."

Hon. Horace N. Congar, lawyer, editor, United States Consul at Hong Kong, China, under President Lincoln; and Consul at Prague, Bohemia, under President Grant:

"United States Consulate,
"PRAGUE, Bohemia.

"There is one thing, my dear Doctor, about your publications which no one can deny. You print your own poetical thoughts and conceptions. They are not copies of some other writer, but stand out clear and distinct with your own diction and strength; written for the scholarly and intelligent, they preserve true simplicity with the real grandeur of their conception."

The Rev. William Hague, D. D. (1808-1887), in "Life Notes; or Fifty Years' Outlook":

"'The (Newark) 'Advertiser' yet lives and thrives, winning to its service the contributions of scholarly writers, among whom we have noticed, occasionally, the veteran physician and poet, Dr. Abraham Coles, author of 'The Evangel' with its immense wealth of critical scholasticism; and the tasteful and rhythmic translator of Latin poetry that enriches our libraries, for instance, in the artistically wrought edition of the 'Dies Iræ.'"

The "Newark Daily Advertiser":

"'The Microcosm' is the only book of the kind in the language, and is well deserving of a place in every library, and might, we think, moreover, be introduced with advantage into all *schools* where *physiology* is taught as an adjunct, if nothing else, to stimulate interest, and relieve the dryness of ordinary text books. In lines of flowing and easy verse, the author sets forth with a completeness certainly remarkable, and with great power and beauty the incomparable marvels of structure and function of the human body.

"This poetic mastery, making ductile the most unpromising materials, has had its latest and supreme exemplification in the completion of the unique work, 'The Life and Teachings of Our Lord, in Verse.' 'The Evangel,' forming the first part, appeared in 1874, 'The Light of the World,' forming the second part and completing the work, is now, 1884, first published. * * *

"By common consent the story of the life of Jesus, as told by the four evangelists, is the unmatched masterpiece of literature.

Its literary interest is hardly inferior to its religious. It is pre-eminently classic. The most fervid encomiums have come from infidels and the great literary artists of the world. To taboo it, therefore, as something outside of literature, betrays ignorance and imbecility. Mr. Edwin Arnold has duly celebrated in his poem, 'The Light of Asia,' the Buddhist hero, Prince Siddartha, and has had, it would seem, readers among all classes. The life and teachings of Him who is 'The Light of the World,' and whose fame fills the ages, are surely not less worthy of regard and study by the cultivators of literature. The author has striven, it would seem, to make his book a veritable cyclopædia of religious knowledge, so comprehensive is its scope. It ranges through the Old Testament and the New. An episode in the first part, outlines nearly the whole history of the Jewish people. The poetical proem and the note appended thereto are in effective antagonism to Darwinism and current evolution theories. An elaborate note on 'The Logos' gives an historical summary of the prevailing creeds and christologies from the earliest times.

"It is not too much to say that it is a book deserving of a place beside the New Testament in every household, and cannot fail to be found a valuable help to every reader and student of the sacred Scriptures."

The Rev. George Dana Boardman, D. D.:

"PHILADELPHIA, Pa.

"MY DEAR DOCTOR COLES—Most happy do I count myself in possessing 'The Light of the World.' It has all those same fine characteristics which so richly mark 'The Evangel.' It must be a source of supreme delight to the accomplished author that he has been permitted to complete a work so lofty in design, and so admirable in execution."

Rev. Alfred Spencer Patton, D. D. (1825-1888), author, editor of "The Baptist Weekly," etc.:

"Our good and gifted friend, Dr. Abraham Coles, has every reason to be gratified with the highly complimentary notices by the press, of his last work, 'The Light of the World,' it being the second volume or completion of his life of Jesus, as told by the evangelists."

The Hon. Joseph P. Bradley, LL. D., one of the Justices of the Supreme Court of the United States:

"WASHINGTON, D. C., Dec. 14, 1884.

"DEAR DOCTOR—I have read nearly all of your beautiful book, 'The Life and Teachings of Our Lord, in Verse,' and like it better the longer I read it. You had two rocks to avoid: on one side *prosaic tameness*, which might be incurred by too rigid an adherence to the text; on the other *rashness* in attempting (even poetical) changes of consecrated forms of expression—changes which no English or American ear would endure. I appreciate the difficulty of the task, and think you have performed it wonderfully well."

John G. Whittier:

"AMESBURY, Mass., January, 1885.

"'The Light of the World' I have read with interest. Thy poetical version of the wonderful narrative seems to be conscientiously faithful to the original, while at the same time it successfully interprets some passages which are not clear to the ordinary reader. It will be a helpful book to many, who will realize, for the first time, the true meaning and significance of the Lord's words. I am, with high respect and esteem, thy friend."

The Right Honorable John Bright, M. P., England:

"132 Picadilly, LONDON, April 30, 1885.

"DEAR DR. COLES—When I began to read your volume on 'The Life and Teachings of Christ in Verse,' I thought you had attempted to gild the refined gold, and would fail—as I proceeded in my reading that idea gradually disappeared, and I discovered that you had brought the refined gold together in a manner convenient and useful and deeply interesting. I have read the volume with all its notes, many of which seem to me of great value. I could envy you the learning and the industry that have enabled you to produce this remarkable work. I hope it may have many readers in all countries where our language is spoken."

The Rev. Henry Griggs Weston, D. D., author and editor, President of the Crozer Theological Seminary, Chester, Pennsylvania:

"Your work, 'The Life and Teachings of Our Lord,' is one of the gratifying fruits of the study which the Gospels have received since I first began to inquire for helps to their understanding."

The Rev. Horatius Bonar, D. D.:

"10 Palmerston Road, Grange, EDINBURGH.
* * * * "I am struck with your command of language, and your skill in clothing the simplicities of history with the elegance of poetry. It ('The Life and Teachings of Our Lord in Verse') is no ordinary volume, and your notes are of a very high order indeed—admirably written, and full of philosophical thought and Scriptural research."

The Rev. Alexander McLaren, D. D.:

"MANCHESTER, Eng., Nov. 3, 1885.

"DEAR SIR—I congratulate you on having accomplished with such success a most difficult undertaking; and on having been able to present the inexhaustible life in a form so new and original. I do not know whether I have been most struck by the careful and fine exegetical study, or the graceful versification of your work. I trust it ('The Life and Teachings of Our Lord in Verse') may be useful, not only in attracting the people, which George Herbert thought could be caught with a song, when they would run from a sermon, but may also help lovers of the sermon to see its subject in a new garb."

Adele M. Fielde, missionary at Swatow, China:

"Those whose judgment is of value have given Dr. Coles' translations of the Latin hymns such high praise, that words of commendation from me would appear presumptuous. I am glad, for the world's sake, that the wonderful Latin hymns were written, and that Dr. Coles has so translated them, and I am glad for my own sake that I have them to read. * * * I think Dr. Coles has done an excellent thing for us in his 'Life and Teachings of Our Lord.'"

Elizabeth Clementine Kinney, author and poet, wife of Hon. William Burnet Kinney; and, by her first husband, Edmund B. Stedman, the mother of Edmund Clarence Stedman, the distinguished poet and critic:

"Dr. Coles long ago established a high reputation in both worlds, by his matchless translations of that famous old judgment hymn, the 'Dies Iræ,' and of mediæval hymns, published under the title of 'Old Gems in New Settings;' also by his unique original poem,

'The Microcosm,' which has glorified by immortal verse this mortal body, so fearfully and wonderfully made that every part harmonizes with the poet's song. In 'The Evangel' and 'The Light of the World,' already noticed by 'The Observer,' while conscientiously adhering to the sacred text, Dr. Coles' frequent elaborate notes give freedom to some original suggestions growing out of the author's fifty years' devout study of the Bible. It will be well to heed any proposition brought forward by one who has been so long a reverent student as to have become a profound thinker, and thus an able teacher of the divine word. Every thought or idea advanced by Dr. Coles will, doubtless, on thorough, unprejudiced investigation, be found supported by a reasonable interpretation of Scripture. Between the acts of this sacred drama there are also some hymnal excursions, which show the height and depth, the color and light, the melody and ecstasy, of the true Christian poet. Through his many works, one noble aim is ever apparent, viz.: to 'crown Him Lord of all' who is 'the author and finisher of our faith' and 'the giver of every good and perfect gift.' Noticeable, too, through all, is progression, in respect of enlargement by study and thought; of advancement with advancing years, keeping pace with the age in increasing light so far as it develops heavenly truth, and original conception through truth."

"The Book Buyer," Charles Scribner's Sons, New York:

"'The Hebrew Psalms in English Verse.' By Abraham Coles, M. D., LL.D. Dr. Coles has won praise from some of the most eminent of critics for his translations into English of the 'Dies Iræ,' the characteristics of the work being faithfulness to the spirit of the original, combined with a command of rich and rythmic English. His tastes have led him to translate the great Hebrew classic into English verse, a task of unusual difficulty which many have undertaken, but in which few have attained even partial success. Dr. Coles's work will attract wide attention by reason of its lofty religious spirit, its admirable reflection of the incomparably fine flavor of the original, its dignified, stately diction and the scholarly care bestowed upon every line. The book, moreover, has an additional value in the prefatory matter which includes an essay on the character of the Psalms, a detailed account of the French, English and Scotch metrical versions of the Psalms and a chapter of interesting notes, critical, historical and biographical. An admirable steel portrait of Dr. Coles serves as a frontispiece to the book."

Rev. Theodore L. Cuyler, D. D., LL. D.:

"DEAR DR. COLES—Your volume on the Psalms is a noble work, and the introduction is rich and sweet as a honeycomb. Two Sabbaths ago I gave out from my pulpit your fine hymn, 'Lo, I am with you all the days,' and told the congregation some things about the author. * * * * You will be quite at home up among heaven's choir of psalmists and chosen singers."

The "New York Tribune":

"'A New Rendering of the Hebrew Psalms into English Verse, with Notes, Critical, Historical and Biographical, including an Historical Sketch of the French, English and Scotch Metrical Versions,' by Dr. Abraham Coles. Dr. Coles' name on the title-page is a sufficient indication of the excellence and thoroughness of the work done. Indeed, Dr. Coles has done much more than produce a fresh, vigorous and harmonious version of the Psalms, though this was alone well worth doing. His full and scholarly notes on the early versions of Clement Marot, Sternhold and Hopkins and others, his sketches of eminent persons connected in various ways with particular psalms, his literary and bibliographical information, together impart a value and interest to this work which should insure an extensive circulation for it. Very much of the historical and other matter thus brought within the reach of the public is inaccessible to such as have not means of access to public libraries, and there is certainly no Christian household in the country which would not find both pleasure and instruction in Dr. Coles' compendious and altogether unique volume. It may be added that in his version of the Psalms he has wisely preserved the rhythmical swing and the terse language which distinguish the early renderings, and that therefore those who have been reared on the old versions need not fear finding their favorites changed 'out of knowledge.'"

The Rev. Frederic W. Farrar, D. D., F. R. S., Chaplain in Ordinary to the Queen, author of the "Life of Christ," etc., in a letter to Dr. Coles:

"17, Dean's Yard, WESTMINSTER, S. W.
"The task of versifying the Psalms was too much even for Milton, but you have attempted it with seriousness and with as much success as seems to be possible. I was much interested in your introduction."

The Rev. A. H. Tuttle, D. D., pastor of the First Methodist Episcopal Church, Wilkesbarre, Pa.:

"'The Life and Teachings of Our Lord, in verse,' has greatly aided me in my efforts to interpret heavenly things. I am glad you have lived to complete your versification of the Psalms. I am now making a protracted and careful study of the old Hebrew Hymn Book, and your work will be of untold help to me. I have already read my favorite psalms as you sing them. They are rich beyond expression."

The Rev. Charles S. Robinson, D. D.:

"I have read many of your really excellent versions of the Psalms. It seems to me you have added richly to our available literature in that direction. I have been specially interested, also, in the prefaced notes. Some of the information is quite new to me, and the comments are all good and helpful."

Hon. George Hay Stuart, the eminent philanthropist in January, 1888, wrote from Philadelphia:

"'The New Rendering of the Hebrew Psalms into English Verse,' I prize very much. It is exceedingly good and very suggestive. The subject matter is of peculiar interest to me. I have been brought up, as perhaps you know, in old Rouse's version of the Psalms, but never held the view, that many do, that nothing else can be sung in the praise of God. Our own congregation, up to recently, used nothing but that version. Now we have so far advanced that we sing, also, hymns and spiritual songs. * * * * The United Presbyterian Assembly has recently adopted a new version of the Psalms, but I think their leading men ought to see this version."

The Rev. D. R. Frazer, D. D., pastor of the First Presbyterian Church, of Newark, N. J.:

"MY DEAR DR. COLES—I do not know that I can give any better expression of my appreciation of your last work than to say that my wife and I sat up until after midnight, reading psalm after psalm with very great delight. The versification is beautiful, and its beauty intensifies by its fidelity to the common version. Hoping the book may do much good, in making manifest the beauties of one of the most beautiful portions of the Word of God, I am, with great respect, ever sincerely yours."

Charles M. Davis, Secretary of the American Institute of Christian Philosophy, Superintendent of Public Schools, Essex county, N. J., etc.:

"DEAR DR. COLES—During the past year I have been reading the revised version of the Psalms, in connection with the received. Your translations will be a help to me, as I do not understand Hebrew. I have read your introduction very carefully, and find it contains especially valuable information, as do, also, your occasional notes. The psalms that I have read aloud in the family have been greatly enjoyed, especially the 107th, 136th and 137th. We are anticipating much pleasure from the continuance of this during the winter evenings."

The Rev. A. H. Lewis, D. D., editor of "The Outlook and Sabbath Quarterly":

"I have been greatly interested in the book, not only in the success which you have attained in versifying the Psalms, but in the valuable matter embodied in the introduction. I have usually found it difficult to interest myself in any versification of the Psalms, especially in the early efforts by Watts and others. On opening your volume, I found myself inclined to read in detail, rather than to examine cursorily. It is very difficult to versify Hebrew poetry. The success you have attained in expressing the delicate shades of sentiment commands our congratulations, and may justly give you abundant satisfaction."

S. W. Kershaw, F. S. A., author, librarian of the Lambeth Palace Library, London, England, etc.:

"LAMBETH LIBRARY, 12 June, 1888.

"* * * * In this library there is a fine collection of works on the liturgies, prayer-book, etc. In your 'New Rendering of the

Hebrew Psalms Into English Verse,' I am greatly interested in the introduction, in reading about the psalms of Clement Marot, and in the allusion to the Huguenots. My little book on the 'Protestants from France in their English home' was kindly reviewed in one of your papers. * * * *"

J. K. Hoyt, editor and author:

"BAY VIEW, Florida.

"DEAR DR. COLES—I have passed a very pleasant Sunday morning in looking over your new book. I wish you had invoked the spirit of Beethoven, and written the music as well as the words; for the proper use of a metrical version of the Psalms is to sing them. Still, the book is a wonderful one, and encourages me to believe that age is not necessarily a bar to work. I enjoy the notes much, and very often find myself turning from the essay to the verses referred to. You will leave a melodious monument behind you, my good Doctor."

The Rev. George Dana Boardman, D. D.:

"MY DEAR DR. COLES—I greatly admire your new book for many reasons: first, for its rich introduction, felicitously describing the character of the Psalms, giving us an exhaustive history of metrical versions, presenting critical, historical and biographical notes of great value; secondly, for your new rendering of the Psalms, a rendering conscientious, mellifluous, fresh and suggestive; thirdly, and not least, for the frontispiece, representing one who has both the David spirit and the David music. Faithfully yours."

The Rev. Lewis R. Dunn, D. D.:

"I like the 'rhythmic flow' of the words of your work, its truths, its thorough orthodoxy, its blending of the results of most recent scholarship in lines and notes, its beautiful illustrations of the text, and its high intellectual and spiritual tone—a classic in our good old English tongue."

Asahel Clark Kendrick, D. D., LL. D., author, Professor of Hebrew, Greek and Latin in the University of Rochester, New York:

"In your translation of the Hebrew Psalms into English verse, you may well be congratulated in having thus nobly crowned your series of poems devoted to those themes, which aid the aspirations of the soul upward toward God and heaven, and may well task the highest human efforts. The renderings are in clear and weighty verse, fitted to the noble simplicity of the original; and the notes are instructive and valuable."

George MacDonald, author and poet:

"LONDON, England.

"MY DEAR DOCTOR COLES.—I send you by this post a copy of my little book on the religious poetry of England. I am sure you will find a good deal to sympathize with in it. * * * I am sorry to say I have not yet received your book, which I should like much to see after the taste you gave me, sheltered and ministered unto by you and yours. Let me hope I may once more be your guest, and that you may be ours. Believe in my love and gratitude. Yours, with sincere affection."

The Rev. Philip Schaff, D. D., LL. D., in "Literature and Poetry," Charles Scribner's Sons, New York, 1890:

"A physician, Abraham Coles, prepared between 1847 and 1859 thirteen versions (of the 'Dies Iræ'), six of which are in the trochaic measure and double rhyme of the original, five in the same rhythm, but in single rhyme, one in iambic triplets, like Roscommon's, the last in quatrains, like Crashaw's version. Two appeared anonymously in the Newark 'Daily Advertiser,' the first one in 1847, and a part of it found its way into Mrs. Stowe's 'Uncle Tom's Cabin;' subsequently this version was set to music in Henry Ward Beecher's 'Plymouth Collection of Hymns and Tunes.' The thirteen versions were first published together with an introduction in 1859. He has since published three additional versions in double rhyme, New York, 1881, in 'The Microcosm and Other Poems.' In August, 1889, he made one more version in single rhyme and four lines. These seventeen versions show a rare fertility and versatility, and illustrate the possibilities of variation, without altering the sense. Dr. Coles, in the eleventh stanza of his first translation of 1847, had anticipated Irons, Périès, and Dix:

> "'Righteous Judge of retribution,
> Make me gift of absolution
> Ere that day of execution.'

* * * "Dr. Abraham Coles, of Scotch Plains, N. J., the successful translator of 'Dies Iræ,' and 'Stabat Mater,' has reproduced, but has not yet (1889), published, all the passion hymns of St. Bernard."

www.ingramcontent.com/pod-product-compliance
Lightning Source LLC
Chambersburg PA
CBHW032043220426
43664CB00008B/845